Call-out

To my companions on rescues,
and especially to the members of
the Glencoe Mountain Rescue Team.

Call-out

A climber's tales of mountain rescue in Scotland

HAMISH MACINNES

Vertebrate Publishing, Sheffield
www.v-publishing.co.uk

Call-out

Hamish MacInnes

 Vertebrate Publishing
Crescent House, 228 Psalter Lane, Sheffield S11 8UT, United Kingdom
www.v-publishing.co.uk

First published in Great Britain in 1973 by Hodder and Stoughton.
This edition first published in 2016 by Vertebrate Publishing.

Cover photo: Rescue dog and chopper. Copyright © John Cleare.
Photography: Hamish MacInnes collection unless otherwise credited.

Hamish MacInnes has asserted his rights under the Copyright, Designs and Patents Act 1988
to be identified as the author of this work.

This book is a work of non-fiction based on the life, experiences and recollections of Hamish MacInnes.
In some limited cases the names of people, places, dates and sequences or the detail of events have
been changed solely to protect the privacy of others. The author has stated to the publishers that, except
in such minor respects not affecting the substantial accuracy of the work, the contents of the book are true.

A CIP catalogue record for this book is available from the British Library.

ISBN 978-1-911342-21-2 (Paperback)
ISBN 978-1-910240-90-8 (ebook)

Every effort has been made to obtain the necessary permissions with reference to copyright material,
both illustrative and quoted. We apologise for any omissions in this respect and will be pleased to make
the appropriate acknowledgements in any future edition.

Produced by Vertebrate Publishing.
Printed and bound by Lightning Source.

Contents

The rocks that roughly handle us,
The peaks that will not go –
The uniformly scandalous
Condition of the snow.

Anon.

Preface to the 1977 Edition

There have been few changes in Glencoe over the years. Apart from the road and a handful of cottages, I suppose it has altered little since the days of the Massacre. The team is still rescuing, and there is the same camaraderie and spirit amongst its members. Occasionally we suffer a loss when someone moves away from the district, but there remains always a healthy nucleus of dedicated volunteers.

Inevitably, money is still short for buying and replacing equipment, though there is now more assistance from the local authorities. Greater use is also being made of helicopters, following the modern trend, as in other countries, of increased mechanisation. But I can't ever see the Glencoe rescue team being out of work, the mountains will see to that!

In recent years there has been a change of emphasis in the accident pattern, an increase in actual climbing injuries and fatalities, as opposed to what we term 'bumbly' call-outs – rescues involving hillwalkers and tourists. But one is occasionally disconcerted to discover that the 'victim' of a call-out has suffered no greater injury than cramp. This is perhaps the fault of well-meaning institutions which, churning out the modern product known as 'climber', have advocated safety at all costs. A thin mist, or a sprained wrist, results in an appeal to the local rescue team. This mode of conduct is to be deplored; the mountaineering my generation grew up to know was a sport of self-reliance.

Only a decade ago it was considered a disgrace to fall off a route; now, with new and improved belaying techniques, this is becoming commonplace in climbers who exceed their capabilities. Inevitably, technical climbing accidents are on the increase. Twenty years ago there were no rescue teams in the remoter regions of Scotland. But times have changed, and I sometimes suspect that in certain areas there are more rescuers than climbers!

We seem to be unlucky with accidents to team members. Dave Knowles, a recently fledged member of the team, was killed by a rock fall on the Eiger. Not only was Dave one of the most willing rescuers we ever had, but he was also a talented mountaineering instructor.

Though some of us may be getting a bit long in the tooth, the younger members have yet to leave us behind. At a recent get-together, Willie Elliot, who had just returned from a meeting with the chief constable, summed it up as he announced proudly, 'Aye, we're now insured for mountain rescue until we reach sixty-five!'

Introduction

Anyone who is unfortunate enough to have an accident on the British hills is liable to be criticised for endangering the lives of those who go out to rescue him. But in all the years that I have been engaged in mountain rescue, although on occasion the rescuer is exposed to danger, I cannot recall a single complaint from a fellow rescuer arising out of concern for his personal safety – risk is an essential element in the nature of this work. There is no doubt that, in winter conditions, mountain rescue in parts of Scotland can be as hazardous as anywhere in the world. Though the mountains are not very high, nevertheless they can be subjected to blizzards and winds of incredible severity, such as are rarely experienced outside the Arctic regions. There have been surprisingly few accidents to rescue-team members on actual rescues, but we have been lucky; I can recall dozens of occasions when every member of the party was exposed to grave danger.

Mountain-rescue work is therefore closely akin to that of the lifeboat service. The elements are the common enemy; saving of life is the common aim. Rescue on the mountains, as at sea, is very much a team operation. Members work in harmony, each performing his allotted task to the best of his ability. Although this book is mainly about my personal experiences, it is written in appreciation of my colleagues, for without them there would be no rescue service in Scotland.

The mountain-rescue organisation in Scotland is fairly complex, since there are three separate bodies involved. Firstly, there are the local teams which now undertake most of the rescue work and are usually unpaid volunteers – shepherds, farmers and climbers, living in the area. These teams rely mainly on charity for their finance, donations from grateful casualties and money from entertainments – concerts and dances – organised by team members, though a certain amount is sometimes received from government sources in the form of an annual grant. During the period that this book covers, these teams were in dire financial straits; sometimes there was not even enough money to pay for torch batteries! The position is gradually improving, but only, I must add, after many people have perished on the hills and the plight of these teams has been publicised by the national press.

Secondly, there are the military mountain-rescue teams. For many years the RAF teams formed the backbone of mountain rescue in Scotland and numerous climbers owe a debt of gratitude to them. Gradually, with the formation of civilian rescue teams in mountainous regions, the RAF have modified their role and now provide support for local teams, particularly on protracted rescues and searches. Their usefulness is by no means diminished, however, and it will be a sad day when the ministry decides to disband them, for though their primary task is to locate crashed aircraft on the mountains, their secondary task – helping with mountain accidents and searches – is a very worthwhile one.

The third body involved in rescue work on the hills is the police. The police in Scotland have always taken an active interest in mountain accidents, much more so than their counterparts in England and Wales. Whether this keen participation is a good thing is open to question; anyone reading this book will inevitably come to the conclusion that a mountain rescuer should first and foremost be a mountaineer, whether he is shepherd or farmer (such men are mountaineers in the true sense of the word), and that 'instant' climbers cannot be created by issuing up-to-date equipment to inexperienced men. But, be that as it may, the police have a vital task to perform in mountain rescue, in a secondary supporting role, in the provision of communications and also in an official capacity, since the possibility of foul play cannot be overlooked in mountain accidents.

In Glencoe we have two rescue groups: the Glencoe Mountain Rescue Team and the Argyll Police Team. There are about twelve members in our local team, which forms the advance group on rescues. The men come from many different walks of life. There is Huan Findlay, for example, six feet three inches tall and a sheep farmer who lives in the heart of Glencoe and was at one time a tea planter in Bhutan. There is Rory MacDonald, the proprietor of the Clachaig Inn; though not a climber he always keeps remarkably fit and, on a rescue, invariably has a half-bottle of whisky in his hip pocket to dispense to the team. John Grey owns a fishing boat and has probably survived more hair-raising episodes on the west coast of Scotland than any man alive. On the hills he is a competent rescuer with a natural aptitude for climbing. Living near him, just south of Glencoe, is John Arthur, a farmer and skier and a pillar of strength. Then there are the local climbers, men such as John and Richard Grieve, John Hardy and Wall Thompson, who are part-time climbing instructors – all mountaineers of the highest calibre. The strength, speed, and competence on the hills of men like Wall Thompson has to be seen to be appreciated, Denis Barclay, an electrician, is one of the founder members of the group. He enjoys a good rescue as much as he enjoys a good pipe, and wears a permanent smile upon his face; after fourteen years of rescuing in Glencoe, he still shows the same enthusiasm towards helping climbers in distress. Then there is Major Eric Moss. Owing to insurance difficulties, Eric was retired from the police team at the age of sixty. Since, by some means, he managed to obtain his own insurance cover for rescuing until his seventieth birthday, we took him under the wing of our local team. Eric is a truly remarkable character; he is amazingly fit for his age and practises running to keep himself in trim. As a piper and composer, he forms the mainstay of our rescue team's musical aspirations. A certain dry brand of humour that he possesses was well illustrated on a recent rescue – rocks were cascading down on our party but Eric didn't flinch. When asked why he didn't run for cover, his reply was 'a rolling stone gathers no moss!' Living in a small, whitewashed cottage under the forbidding face of Aonach Dubh are the Elliot brothers. Walter and Willie were engaged in rescue work in the glen before any of us. Following the example set by their father, they have helped to take the injured and dead off the Glencoe hills since they were seventeen years old, and are still as active as ever. There are very few families in Britain who have done so much in the public cause.

The Argyll police team is led by Sandy Whillans, now our local police sergeant. Affectionately known as Sandy, he has been associated with us since he came to Kinlochleven as a young constable, many years ago. I must say that rescues seem dull when Sandy isn't with us – although that is a rare occurrence! He has an incorrigible sense of humour and, on a rescue, his boisterous laughter echoes like thunder round the corries. Sandy is a great family man and the deaths of young people on our hills always have a profound effect on him; like the rest of us, he hates to see lives thrown away unnecessarily. There are also one or two local chaps who are enrolled as special constables and help the police team during rescues: Alasdair MacDonald, a gamekeeper, and his brother-in-law Cecil MacFarlane, who is a rescue-dog handler.

We have, besides, many transient helpers in the team. Climbing instructors for my 'snow and ice' climbing courses usually play an important part in rescues; likewise, other climbers who happen to be living in the glen – even those only visiting – are often pressed into service. Some reference should also be made to the Search and Rescue Dog Association, for this organisation plays an important part in search work in the Highlands and, indeed, throughout Britain. Dog handlers are usually team members whose dogs are trained to find people buried under avalanches or lying out in open country, in both summer and winter. Again, it is a voluntary body; each winter an annual training course is based at Kings House Hotel, Glencoe.

An active interest in mountain-rescue work is bound to promote a 'canny' respect for the hills, but rescuers are by no means infallible. Twice in my own climbing career my more accustomed role has been reversed and I have found myself on the 'receiving' end of a rescue. The first occasion was during an early attempt on Raven's Gully in Glencoe. Sixty feet from the top of this difficult climb, the rope had jammed below me. I was then climbing with two friends;

as they weren't able to climb up to me and I had no place to secure my rope, I had the alternatives of staying where I was – the two front points of my crampons resting on a small foothold – or untying and going on up. I decided on the latter course. Six feet from the top of the route, I got stuck in a difficult, iced-up chimney. It was dark by now, but my companions realised the seriousness of my predicament and signalled for help with their torches. Several ace 'tigers' rushed up another route to the summit of the mountain, then descended to the top of the gully. Eventually I received a top rope at 2.50 a.m., after I had been balanced on the front points of my crampons for over eight hours, dressed only in jeans and a tartan shirt since my spare clothing was in my friend's rucksack!

My other 'unfortunate' incident occurred in the French Alps, where, as a young man, I used to follow the well-known climber Lionel Terray. We had an arrangement whereby I would follow him 'solo' while he climbed with a client. This meant that I didn't have the difficulty of route finding – a major problem for British climbers with limited time at their disposal. Lionel used to call me jokingly the 'guideless Aberdonian'.

I had completed the traverse of the Grands Charmoz with him – a respectable hundred feet or so behind his client – and we all enjoyed a snack on the summit. On the descent, Lionel abseiled from a nylon tape sling which was already fastened round a rock bollard. The shortcomings of these slings, when exposed to excessive ultraviolet light, wasn't widely recognised at that time. I sunned myself on a ledge above as they descended from the rock belay down a vertical wall. It was forty feet in height and terminated in a small ledge; from this point the steep wall continued sheer for another 600 feet down to the glacier.

Without a second thought I put my doubled rope through the sling. I had just allowed my full weight to bear on the sling when I found myself dropping – I didn't know what had happened as I plunged downwards. I struck the ledge below with great force and my legs doubled up underneath me, as if driven by a hydraulic ram. Like a jackknife closing, my knees made contact with my eyes with a force which blinded me. Lionel must have heard my shout and climbed up to me instantly. He dragged me away from the edge of the ledge where I had providentially ended my lightning descent. Just at that moment he saw his friend, Raymond Lambert, the famous guide, coming down the face of the Grépon and called for his assistance. Raymond's companion, a trainee guide, went down the mountain to seek further help. With the assistance of these two famous climbers I managed to climb down, facing into the hill since both my heels were damaged and I was unable to see. Fortunately, the injuries I sustained were light for such a fall and I was back climbing in a month or so.

I have mentioned these two instances to illustrate that rescuers, too, can well appreciate what is involved for both patient and rescuer.

We are often asked why we go out on rescues. The answer is simple – we cannot, even if we feel so inclined, leave people stranded or injured on the hills, any more than we can ignore a car accident on the road. Not all the people involved in mountain accidents are stupid. Accidents occur in the mountains just as they do anywhere else, and I don't consider it our place to stand in judgement of our fellows. Besides, even if the casualty is guilty of negligence, the experience of an accident is generally chastisement enough. Occasionally, if the basic rules of safety have been blatantly ignored, this must be pointed out, but happily these instances are becoming less frequent and anyone making such criticism should have a very wide knowledge of both mountaineering and rescue work.

I would like to conclude this introduction by saying that some of my most memorable recollections of the mountains are of rescues. On an exacting rescue each moment is remembered with amazing clarity, for one lives at a higher pitch than usual when risks must be taken which wouldn't normally be contemplated. Only too often it is a fight for life: there is nothing more satisfying than the successful evacuation of a critically injured person on a highly technical rescue, where a single mistake could result in death for the casualty. It is, on a grand scale, a game of chance in which nature holds most of the cards.

1   The Thousand-foot Fall

It had been snowing all day in the lower part of Glencoe, providing a heavy new cover; even down at my house the snowflakes were now falling steadily. Visibility was restricted to a line along the base of the mountains and only occasionally did we catch fleeting glimpses of the steep faces of the peaks opposite.

I was speaking to Willie Elliot, who had been up shooting hinds close to the road above the gorge. Willie, as well as being a self-employed sheep farmer, is also the part-time National Trust employee in the glen. Some of his work entails taking clients stalking in the autumn and, also, culling hinds during the winter months.

Willie had called in at my workshop on his way back home.

'Aye, it's gie coorse,' he remarked, stamping the snow off his boots. 'I wouldn't like to be on the peaks today.'

'Well, at least it should keep climbers off the hills.' No sooner had I said this than we observed two snow-encrusted figures staggering down the hillside above my house.

'I'm not so sure,' he answered. 'Look at these blokes.'

'They'll never learn; all they need to do is to sprain an ankle and their little excursion could develop into an epic.'

Willie was naturally well aware of this; he, his brother Walter, and their father, now dead, had been out on so many rescues that they must have lost count of them years ago. Willie and Walter's first recollection of a rescue was in 1934 when they were small boys. They were huddled in a corner of their house – Achnambeithach – when an unconscious climber was brought in on a stretcher after a difficult rescue. The casualty was put in an adjoining room where Mrs Elliot had made up a camp bed. The injured man, a Mr Ian Campbell, a solicitor from Edinburgh, had fallen off the Church Door Buttress of Bidean nam Bian and had been rescued by some of his friends and Mr Elliot.

In those days there were no telephones in Glencoe. These were not installed in the glen until Mr Ernest Marples – one-time postmaster-general and an active climber – had a line put up through the glen from Glencoe village to Kings House Hotel in the early 1950s. In an emergency such as this one, Mr Elliot would get on his bicycle and pedal up to Achtriochtan Farm to call out the Marquises, then travel several miles down the road to Achnacon to call out the Browns, finally riding up the narrow track to Gleann-leacna-muidh to alert Mr Aitchison, the farmer. If it was going to be a long rescue other helpers had to be rounded up from the village.

Mrs Elliot recalls quite vividly that first rescue in Glencoe: apparently Mr Stark, the factor, went in to have a look at Campbell in the other room. He then came into the living room where she was handing out bowls of soup to the exhausted rescuers who were gathered round the blazing fire. Steam was rising from their wet clothes as the fresh, melting snow fell to the floor.

'There's no need for your camp bed, Mrs Elliot,' said the factor. 'I'm afraid he's gone.'

A silence fell in the room which was only broken by the arrival of Dr Grant, the local doctor. In a few minutes he told them that Campbell was still alive, though deeply unconscious; he was taken to hospital and remained in this state for the next three weeks. When he eventually regained consciousness he waved his arms about violently as he came round: the nurse at his bedside asked him what he was doing.

'Oh, I thought I was coming through the Church Door,' were his first words.

In those days there was very little rescue gear in the glen and the local shepherds cherished all they had, for there was little spare cash available to buy such luxuries as ropes and special boots. One of Mr Elliot's prize possessions was a German storm lantern which, he maintained, would stay alight in any wind. On one rescue he was separated from this coveted item of equipment and never saw it again – a common enough occurrence even on rescues today. He bemoaned this sad loss to many, vowing that he would never find another like it. During the next few months, as friends and climbers heard of his loss, new storm lanterns in all shapes and sizes arrived by post at the cottage. Every stormy night for months afterwards Mr Elliot, or one of his sons, would go outside to test the latest acquisition, but it was always the same – none ever matched up to the lost one!

'There must be quite an avalanche risk today,' observed Willie, peering from the doorway up into the Lost Valley.

'No doubt about that. There's a hard underlayer from that last frost – just before the New Year – and now at least two feet of fresh snow is lying on top. There won't be much to hold it in the steeper gullies.'

'Well, I must go,' he said. 'I hope we're not out today, that's all I say.'

I said 'cheerio' and he went off in his Morris Traveller, sliding slightly as he took the corner below the house.

Up behind the workshop a large herd of hinds had gathered and from across the river came the roar of a stag. The sheep stood in dejected groups, snow sticking to their fleeces, and the county council snowploughs were having difficulty in keeping the road open.

There were a lot of climbers in the glen that January weekend, snow and fair weather proving strong incentives for their activities. The local pubs were busy all evening as climbers returned off the hill.

I had just written a few letters after dinner and was talking to some friends when the telephone rang. It was Doris Elliot, Willie's sister, who is the receptionist at Kings House Hotel.

'Hello, Hamish,' she began. 'There's been an accident on the Buachaille. Three chaps had a fall in Crowberry Gully.'

'Are there any survivors there?' I asked.

'Yes, there's a chap here, his name is David Tod. Do you want to speak to him?'

'Please, Doris.'

I remembered David as a slim, ginger-haired youth who came up to the glen fairly often.

'Hello, Hamish. We had a fall from the last pitch of Crowberry. One of the lads is still up there.'

'Look, Dave,' I interrupted, realising the urgency. 'If you can get down to Jacksonville I'll meet you as soon as possible. I'll get the full story there.'

'Right, I'll be there,' he replied.

Jacksonville is a mountain bothy built by members of the Creagh Dhu Mountaineering Club and is situated by the river at the base of Buachaille Etive Mor, the Big Herdsman, of Glen Etive. I was with the Creagh Dhu that sublime June day in 1950 when the first Jacksonville was built by Jimmy Jackson, a member of the Club. Since that time it has been the exclusive living-quarters of these hard climbers and, though it is never locked up, no climber has yet had the temerity to stay there uninvited, so powerful is the reputation of the Creagh Dhu. Other pastimes of the club include wrestling and weightlifting; this factor, added to a background of living in the heart of Glasgow, has led to a widespread respect for their resourcefulness in brawls and other 'momentous' encounters.

Before I left the house I called out the team, suggesting that we should meet at Jacksonville. The tale of the accident, which Dave Tod delivered that night by the dim light of two candles in Jacksonville, was a remarkable one, to say the least.

The party – David Tod, Robert Gow and Neil Keith – was ascending an ice pitch of Crowberry Gully, which leads almost to the summit of the mountain, when Bob Gow, who was coming up last, came off. He fell, pulling his friends with him. Their ice-axe belay – seldom satisfactory – came out. They shot down the gully, which resembles a narrow alleyway cut into the solid rhyolite of the mountain at an angle of some forty-five degrees; this is interspersed with abrupt ice pitches. It doesn't run in a straight line but twists and turns, hemmed in by the massive gully walls, at times only a few feet in width.

I don't suppose we will ever know the speed that this party reached during their 1,000-foot fall but it must have been breathtaking. They passed the point where the gully forks – the scene of many other rescues – in a huge wave of snow, then shot down a long straight section of the gully where the true right wall leans over the gully bed, hiding it from the road. Their headlong descent continued over some steep pitches, now filled up with fresh snow; fortunately, each collision they had with the gully walls and buried rocks was cushioned by hundreds of tons of snow.

Eventually, they rocketed out of the base of the gully, which separates the huge walls of Crowberry Ridge on one side and the massive cliff of North Buttress on the other, and continued down towards the lower slopes of the mountain. They were heading for some more vertical drops near the top of the Waterslab, a smooth sweep of rock situated where the path from Jacksonville steepens on the lower slopes. Bob Gow, who was falling first, shot down the true continuation of Crowberry Gully, while Dave and Neil went down a subsidiary steep funnel of ice. The No. 2 Viking nylon rope to which they had been tied has a minimum breaking-strain of 3,000 pounds and they were still roped up. As the rope suddenly tightened Neil and Dave came to rest with a sickening jerk. Dave was halfway down the ice scoop and Neil was dangling on the end over a vertical drop. With great difficulty, using his last ounce of strength, Dave untied himself with bare hands and pulled Neil into the face so that he could untie him. They were now actually on the access path, almost at the foot of the mountain – their fall must forever remain the fastest descent of Buachaille Etive Mor.

Somewhere above them lay Bob Gow. With a tremendous effort, considering the shock of the fall, Dave climbed up to where the rope had snagged, but in his exhausted state, with no equipment, he had to give up; he couldn't see any sign of Gow and there was no response to his calls. Neil was injured and in urgent need of medical attention, so they both staggered like drunks down through the deep snow, numbed by the fall and fatigue and the terrible knowledge that their friend lay above yet they were unable to help him. They reached their small tent near Coupal Bridge eventually. Dave forced himself to keep going to Kings House Hotel.

We listened to this tale while outside the snow still fell heavily. A shout from across the river heralded the arrival of Sandy Whillans and some of the rescue team.

John (Big) Maclean and David Agnew were the only Creagh Dhu residents in Jacksonville that night. Big John had been on many rescues with us in the past and could always be relied upon for his prodigious strength and climbing ability, for he was one of the best climbers in Scotland. David Agnew was then a young man as broad as he was tall; a fine wrestler and weightlifter, at that time a frequent climber in Glencoe.

'Aye, Dave and Neil were bloody lucky,' said Big Maclean to me. 'They're no bad climbers.'

In John's language this meant that they were very good. As a matter of fact, Dave was later to join the Creagh Dhu and lived up to Maclean's estimation of his ability.

'Well,' I said, 'I think we'd better make a move.' I turned to Sandy who was squatting beside me. 'We'll have to keep everyone off the hill. If we don't we'll surely lose someone. It'll be a deathtrap up there tonight.' I jerked a thumb in the direction of Buachaille.

'I'll get a couple of the police to keep everyone down below.'

'Fine. It'd be as well if John, Davy Agnew and yourself came up with me. That'll be enough to determine if he's still alive and we can take a stretcher and casualty bag up with us. We should manage to get him off on our own.'

It was fortunate that we all knew the Buachaille like the backs of our hands, otherwise we would never even have reached the bottom of the Waterslab that night. Our headlamps could only pick out the snow-covered heather a short way ahead and large flakes of snow fell as persistently as ever. We had been told that it had started snowing heavily up here at about 4 p.m.

'What a bloody night,' muttered Davy from behind, struggling with the stretcher; those of us who were lighter laden led, forcing a trail through the snow. We paused beneath the bottom of the Waterslab, where a great column of ice rose vertically to the overhanging nose of this long sweep of iced rock.

Sandy had his pipe lit. 'I don't like the look of this, Hamish,' he said. 'I'll be very surprised if he's still alive.'

'I think you're right,' I agreed. 'It would be a miracle indeed if all three survived such a fall.'

'Aye,' interjected John. 'This beats Bill Smith's fall from Raven's Gully, Hamish. That time you were up with him, he fell all of 500 feet, didn't he, and wasn't he still okay after that?'

'Yes, that's right. We were attempting the first winter ascent and were above pitch four when the ice gave way underneath him. He shot away down into Great Gully and shouted back, "Come on doon – it's great!"'

Always when there is an excessive snowfall, as there was on that bleak night in January 1961, there is a very high avalanche risk. It is now common practice throughout mountainous regions to issue avalanche warnings as soon as the snowfall exceeds twelve inches (thirty centimetres). Where we stood at the base of the Waterslab, the snow was at least two feet deep! To make matters still more hazardous, the old snow in the gullies, which had fallen before the New Year was iron-hard and the numerous boulders and crannies, which might have afforded some anchorage to the new snow, were covered and transformed into smooth slopes. Had the snow remained undisturbed, without the surface tension being broken, it would probably have adhered to the gullies and the steep faces, but its instability was such that the disturbance caused by a climber, or even a falling rock, was enough to send it crashing down; a falling mass like this will often trigger off other avalanches on adjoining slopes and gullies. But in 1961 little was known about avalanches in Scotland, and, indeed, in climbing circles generally interest in avalanches was minimal.

We skirted round to the south of the Waterslab and followed, as best we could, the approximate line of the summer path. There was now no sign of the tracks of the two survivors; they had vanished under a smooth, white blanket.

In the beam of my torch I spotted the thread-like rope hanging down the vertical face to our right on the steep face of rock which marks the bottom of Curved Ridge, the one relatively easy way up the front of this precipitous mountain.

'Look – over there – the rope. It's hanging in the place where Snodgrass fell.' (Snodgrass was a Glaswegian climber who sometimes used to come out with the club and who was killed at that spot.)

'Yes, that's it,' said Davy.

A short way below, Davy had given the stretcher to John for a turn at carrying.

'I think I'd better go up with Davy, seeing he's nearest to me,' I said. 'It looks bloody dangerous.'

'Aye, there's no sense in us all being killed; we don't want to depopulate the glen, after all,' answered John with his customary deadpan expression.

'I'm glad MacInnes is up there,' Sandy butted in, 'or he'd be off after venison. Remind me to search his car when I get back, young fella,' he laughed.

Afterwards I told the boys about this remark of Sandy's, 'He must have been bloody psychic – I had a stag in the boot all the time!'

Davy and I put on our crampons and roped up. Ten minutes later we were on the steep, rising traverse leading up to where the rope hung. During a hard winter this section can be tricky even in daylight, but we didn't encounter any real difficulty. Once I got to the frozen rope, I climbed up the ice scoop where it hung, using the rope as a handrail.

'If it held two survivors it'll surely hold us now,' I remarked optimistically.

Reaching the top I discovered that the rope hung down from a point of rock and disappeared into a mass of avalanche debris in the shallow gully below. Beyond this again, I could see, by torchlight, where the snow ended abruptly at the edge of a big drop. There was no sign of Bob Gow.

Securing the safety rope as best I could round a boulder which I cleared of snow, I shouted for Davy to climb. As he came up I looked about me. There was little to see, the snow slopes were visible by the head torch within a range of a few feet; beyond this was an opaque curtain of falling snow. Davy loomed beside me like a ghost.

'I can't see any sign of him, Davy.'

'That's funny. He must be about somewhere.' He shone his lamp over the avalanche debris. 'He must be under this lot; the rope goes under the snow just below us here.'

'Aye, I can see that. If you watch my rope, I'll start digging,' I replied. 'Keep your eyes open for any further avalanches.'

'Too bloody right,' he muttered, taking a strong grip of my rope as I kicked down the hard snow boulders of the avalanche.

The avalanche rip of this Crowberry Gully avalanche wasn't big. The snow boulders were only about ten inches in diameter, but I knew from previous experience that it didn't take much to cover and kill a man. There are few tasks worse than digging for a body in an avalanche tip on a wild winter's night. It is an eerie and unpleasant experience; you are working away, trying to be both quick and careful so that you won't injure the buried man with your ice axe, not knowing what you are going to uncover – a corpse, or a live climber. Snow tends to keep a well-clad body relatively well insulated, while wind has a most treacherous cooling effect, under an avalanche you are well protected from the wind – but you must have air to survive.

I uncovered a boot first, then a lower leg, then another boot. He was hanging head first down the slope under the debris, face down, with a loop of rope snagged round one leg in a half hitch. It seemed to take hours to uncover him. All the while Davy watched my rope and listened for the warning sounds of a further avalanche.

It was 11.30 p.m. before I had him entirely free of the snow. By this time I didn't have much doubt that he was dead. He probably died instantly, as he had head injuries. Davy shouted this news down to Sandy and John, saying that we would either spend the night where we were or come down later.

'Thank Christ we can move at last,' shouted Sandy. 'There are very nearly two other corpses down here now! Be seeing you.' As the snowfall eased momentarily I could see their torches bobbing down the hillside; they were obviously sliding down on their backsides, a sport known to mountaineers as glissading. They had left the stretcher where they had been standing because we would need it the following day to take the body down.

David had come down to join me by the body and we cut a ledge out of the snow where the avalanche had scoured the top layer away. We dropped our rucksacks on this ledge, sat upon them and had some chocolate. The body lay by my right foot, just off our ledge.

'What do you think we should do, Davy?' I asked, handing him a piece of chocolate.

'Buggered if I know. You do have a bivvy sack with you?'

'Yes, it'll hold the two of us; we could be quite comfortable here for the night.'

'Aye, I suppose we could,' he returned meditatively.

Suddenly I stood up. I had a curious feeling of impending disaster. Davy did the same.

'Let's get the hell out of here, Davy,' I yelled, grabbing my rucksack. Without even bothering about the rope, which we had taken off, we ran across the avalanche debris, jumping over the body of Robert. Davy was close on my heels, his crampons crunching into the snow boulders. It seemed such a stupid thing to do, as the section where the survivors' rope hung was a difficult one and to negotiate it without being roped up would have required great care, especially on the descent.

There was no time for such thoughts, however; immediately we heard an ominous sound, a deep roar, like a tube train coming out of a tunnel. Yet another avalanche; I cursed. In seconds it had us in its grip, tossing us like woollen dolls down the slope leading to the vertical drop. We were wrapped in a cold blanket of snow. I remember turning over and over, then everything was quiet; I realised I had stopped, and extricated myself from the avalanche debris. Alongside me I saw the white apparition, which was Davy, newly risen from the depths. We were still alive, we felt our arms, legs, ribs – incredibly we appeared to be uninjured. We had lost everything, our rucksacks, gloves, hats and ice axes. Only our crampons were still attached to our feet. We shook ourselves, unable to believe what had happened; it was as if we had received a severe electric shock.

'Well,' said Davy in a tremulous voice, 'we did say to the lads that we might be back, didn't we?'

'Aye,' I replied, spitting a mass of snow, which I had half-swallowed, on to the ground. 'A bit sooner than anticipated!'

We had fallen about 170 feet, seventy of them vertical. In summer the base of this cliff is a mass of large boulders, yet there must have been enough snow to cushion our fall; we didn't have a single scratch, but there was snow inside our clothing, even between our underclothes and our skin.

We were now without torches, but we could see a faint gleam of light below – the window of Jacksonville – through the sporadic showers of snow and, to the east, the welcome lights of Kings House Hotel. We took a straight line towards the light and didn't stop until we burst through the low doorway.

Sandy and John were mildly surprised.

'Well, that didn't take you long,' Big John observed. 'We haven't had time to get a brew on yet.'

'Yes, we don't waste much time,' I commented, taking a seat. 'Especially when persuaded by a few hundred tons of snow!' We told them of the avalanche.

'Where's the body now?' asked Sandy, anxious to know the movement of corpses on his beat.

'Blowed if I know,' I replied. 'Have you any idea, Davy?'

'Something hit me before I went over the edge, but I've no idea what it was – could have been a rock.'

'Anyhow, we'll find it in the morning,' I said. 'You may as well stay the night with me, Sandy; there's no point in going all the way round to Kinlochleven.'

'That'll be fine. Have you enough gear to go back up tomorrow?'

'Oh, yes. I've a spare ice axe and other equipment at home. I must see if I can find my gear tomorrow, though.'

After a mug of hot tea I went off with Sandy and a few team members who had remained by the vehicles while we were up the hill. The policeman left on duty at the main-road car park had done a good job in keeping volunteers off the hill; there was now a large crowd around the police Land Rover. The RAF team from Leuchars, Fife, had recently arrived with Bill Rankin, their team leader. We spoke to him before going home, asking if he could join us at first light to go up and recover the body.

'Yes, I'll be there with the lads. We'll probably camp the night down by the loch.'

'Good night,' we chorused as we stepped into my car.

Sandy slept that night on the floor. At 8 a.m. the alarm went off; it seemed as if I had only just closed my eyes. The day was dull and cloudy; though the snow had ceased, angry clouds still hung close about the mountains.

We set off with the RAF party and made good time to the Waterslab. Our tracks from the previous night were still visible. With Sandy, I once again climbed up the traverse line to where we had found the body the previous night. There was no sign of the body now, nor of the rope which had still been attached to it when we were avalanched. Sandy belayed me at precisely the same point as Davy had before and I went down the snow slope, now polished to an even smoother finish by the latest avalanche.

The body had utterly vanished. Some of the RAF chaps had gone to the bottom of the face where we had landed the night before; they shouted up to us: 'We can't see any sign of it down here either.'

As I was climbing back up to Sandy, I saw, half-buried, a section of bloody rope – presumably the one which was still attached to the corpse, since David and I had used a white rope – we had coiled it up and David had been sitting upon it to provide extra insulation on top of his rucksack.

'He must be jammed somewhere down the face,' I called to Sandy. 'I'd better abseil down and see; it's very steep.'

'Okay,' answered Sandy. 'Come back up and we'll fix another rope for you.'

When this rope was attached to a rock belay, I went down over the edge of the face. About fifteen feet down I found the body wedged in a crack. I shouted back to Sandy: 'Keep me tight on the safety rope. I'll try to prise it from the crack.'

This was no easy task and only by levering it out, using my crampons for purchase, did I succeed in freeing it. I watched it drop into the deep snow below, then followed after on the abseil rope.

The RAF team took the body down to the waiting ambulance. We were back at the car park by 2.45 p.m. after suffering a soaking while crossing the river.

This rescue has always stuck in my mind because of its psychic quality: I am unable to explain our actions that bleak night, why we suddenly had an urgent desire to escape from the gully. Perhaps, as some authorities suggest, there is some electrical influence created by an approaching avalanche. I can't recall ever discussing it again with Davy; one simply accepts these things. Even when we met recently in the Yosemite Valley in California, our talk was of what we were going to do and not about the past.

2 Skye: New Year 1963

Over the Christmas period in 1962 there had been a number of rescues in Glencoe and, as I couldn't see any prospect of these decreasing during the New Year celebrations, I thought that a quiet few days in Skye were just what I needed before returning to Glencoe for the remainder of the winter.

I travelled north with my wife Catherine and our dog Tiki on 29 December. There was quite a bit of ice about, but a distinct lack of snow. The further north and west we went, the less we found. At the latitude of Skye, between 570° 44' N. and 570° 03' N., it grows dark very early at that time of year and we needed the car lights by 3 p.m., for the day was overcast and a biting wind was blowing from the north-west.

There is seldom a queue in winter for the ferry from Kyle of Lochalsh to Kyleakin on Skye. After only a brief wait we drove on to the ferry and were soon on our way across to the 'Misty Isle', a crossing which takes just a few minutes. On the Skye side, immediately to the left of the jetty, are the ruins of Caisteal Maol; at one time, it is said, a Norwegian princess stretched a chain from the Caisteal across to the mainland and passing boats had to pay a toll. Indeed, the Vikings ruled these islands of the west for some 500 years and, even today, one can imagine their longships plying their way between the islands of Rùm, Canna and Eigg.

Skye itself is steeped in superstition and romantic history, from Bonnie Prince Charlie to fairy flags and bloody clan feuds; the last battle of the clans was fought here in 1601 in the Corrie of the Spoils (Coire na Creiche) in the Cuillins. These legends are an essential part of the island's peculiar attraction, which is so hard to define. People call it the 'magic' of Skye. Certainly there is a strange compulsion to return to the island once you have visited it and, even after having climbed in the Cuillins for many years, I still feel an expectancy as I drive off the ferry and head for the heart of the Cuillins; there, for me, lies the heart of Skye.

The name Skye is, like the island, shrouded in mystery. Some say it means 'the winged isle'. Indeed, six wings, or fingers, of land stick out into the sea and there are no less than fifteen major sea lochs biting into the island, so that no part of Skye is more than five miles from the sea.

Geologically, the Cuillins of Skye are fascinating. The tertiary volcanic activity consisted mainly of outpourings from several elongated fissures;

these allowed the flow of molten rock from reservoirs deep in the earth's crust and also, possibly, from localised volcanoes. The work of ice, during the Pleistocene Ice Age which started approximately two million years ago and terminated about 10,000 years ago, is clearly to be seen in the great 'glacier corries', the bowls of which were scooped out by the action of the ice. This abrasive work is evident in the smooth, pebble-scratched slabs around Coir' an Lochain.

There are two main ranges in Skye, the Red Hills, which bound the road to the west and south as one travels north from Kyleakin, and, further west still, the great cirque of the Black Cuillins, which forms a wreath around Loch Coruisk. The Red Hills are of granite and their colour becomes most apparent when viewed from the Black Cuillins, looking eastwards. The granite weathers in a much more uniform manner than the gabbro of the Black Cuillins and produces the gentle outlines characteristic of this range.

Disregarding many outriders, the main Cuillin Ridge is about seven miles long. As a mountain range it is unique in the British Isles. A combination of sea and jagged mountain provides for the climber an unsurpassed mountain environment. Within this relatively small area is packed the most exacting and narrowest ridge in Britain.

At one time the centre for climbing was the Sligachan Inn. This is found where the road from Kyleakin forks, one road leading to Portree, the largest town on the island, and the other to Dunvegan and Glen Brittle. Sligachan Inn was the haunt of the Victorian climbers who made many of the first ascents of the Cuillins. Later, when climbing became more popular and climbers more impecunious, the centre of activity moved to Glen Brittle, a valley to the west of the Cuillins which now boasts a youth hostel and a climbers' hut.

In the heart of the Cuillins lies Loch Coruisk, or Coir'-Uisg. Its name is most appropriate, for it means 'the corrie of water'. It is some two miles long and lies among the glacier-worn slabs of lower Coir'-Uisg. Between the south end of Loch Coruisk and Loch Scavaig, close to the shores of the latter, is the Coruisk Hut, a small climbing refuge nestling under a red wall of gabbro and a popular hostelry for climbers wanting peace and quiet – not always found now at the Glen Brittle site where camping can become congested.

The situation is superb at the Coruisk Hut, but in heavy rain and violent weather the place can become a trap, albeit a pleasant one. Return routes to civilisation not involving river crossings are limited, and you can find yourself an involuntary prisoner unless you are prepared to embark on one of the high pass routes back to Glen Brittle.

Sir Walter Scott was obviously very impressed with, his visit to Loch Coruisk. He wrote:

We were now under the western termination of the high ridge of mountains called Cuillen or Quillen or Coolin, whose weather-beaten and serrated peaks we had admired at a distance from Dunvegan. They appeared to consist of precipitous sheets of naked rock, down which the torrents were leaping in a hundred lines of foam. The tops of the ridge, apparently inaccessible to human foot, were rent and split into the most tremendous pinnacles ... From the bottom of the bay [Loch Scavaig] advanced a headland of high rocks, which divided its depth into two recesses, from each of which a brook issued. Here it had been intimated to us that we would find some romantic scenery, but we were uncertain up which inlet we should proceed in search of it. We chose, against our better judgement, the southerly dip of the bay, where we saw a house which might afford us information. We found, upon inquiry, that there is a lake adjoining to each branch of the bay, and walked a couple of miles to see that near a farmhouse, merely because the honest highlander seemed jealous of his own loch, though we were speedily convinced that it was not that which we were recommended to examine ...

We returned and re-embarked in our boat, for our guide shook his head at our proposal to climb over the peninsula, or rocky headland which divides the two lakes. [The path over this headland holds the famous 'Bad Step' or 'Mauvais Pas'.]

Arrived at the depth of the bay we found that the discharge from this second lake forms a sort of waterfall, or rather a rapid stream, which rushes down to the sea with great fury ...

Advancing up this huddling and riotous brook, we found ourselves in a most extraordinary scene; we lost sight of the sea almost immediately after we had climbed over a low ridge of crags, and were surrounded by mountains of naked rock of the boldest and most precipitous character. The ground on which we walked was the margin of a lake, which seemed to have sustained the constant ravage of torrents from these rude neighbours. We proceeded a mile and a half up this deep, dark and solitary lake. The mountain vapours which enveloped the mountain ridges obliged us by assuming a thousand varied shapes, changing their drapery into all sorts of forms, and sometimes clearing off altogether ...

It was along this dark margin of the lake that, on 2 January, in an exhausted condition and in almost total darkness, we were to carry the bodies of three young climbers to Coruisk Hut. However, as we sped down the hill into Glen Brittle, this was still some four days ahead and we looked forward to our arrival at the Campbells at Cuillin Cottage. John Campbell and his wife Allison were old friends of mine. I had first got to know them when I stayed with them for long periods while I was teaching rock climbing on courses that were based at their cottage.

Fortunately, I didn't have much to drink that Hogmanay. Just as well, for two reasons. One was that I had promised John I would prune the high branches of the trees which encircle his cottage; the other was that by nightfall we would be climbing over the main ridge in an endeavour to save the life of a fallen climber.

I had just finished on the last tree, leaving below a mess of tangled, sawn-off branches which John was vainly trying to burn as fast as I cut them.

'Is that enough, John?' I shouted down to him.

'Aye, not a bad trim.' He looked up, pushing his cap back. 'That should do until your next visit.'

'You're obviously not wanting to see me in the near future,' I rejoined. 'These branches won't grow again for five years.'

'Never fear, we'll find something else needing done, no doubt. Are you coming down for a stroupach? [cup of tea].'

'That's the most sensible thing I've heard you saying for some time, John.'

I had just turned round on the stump of the cut-off limb on which I was standing and was preparing to descend, using the climbing rope which I had doubled round the tree trunk higher up, when I glanced up the hill. The Cuillins stood out in dark relief against a still blue sky, cold-looking, with a silvery tinge which denoted more ice than there had been the previous day. By instinct, my eye followed the path down from Coire Làgan which I knew so well. In the past I had frequently scanned it for tired and straggling course members. I saw a blur of movement, then it disappeared. I was just telling myself that I was seeing things when it appeared again, nearer this time. It was a figure running fast down the hillside. I knew from bitter experience that something was wrong.

The runner was quite tall and slimly built. He had with him an ice axe and was clad with the minimum amount of gear for someone off the tops in winter. His face was pale and, as he approached where I stood at the gate, I could smell blood, that stale smell which one who has worked with corpses doesn't forget and recognises instantly.

'There's been an accident,' he gasped. 'Three have fallen at the back of the Dubhs and one is still alive. Colin Stead is still with them.'

'You'd better come in for a minute,' I suggested. 'And tell us the whole story.'

His name was George Wallace and he was leading a party from Glasgow University Mountaineering Club. They had arrived on 29 December at the

Coruisk Hut, by boat from Mallaig. There were several girls in the party and they had enough food with them to ensure that they would be well fed during their holiday. George was from Mallaig; an experienced and, as we subsequently found, very fit mountaineer. He told us over a plate of hot soup that three members of their group, John Roycroft (twenty-eight), John Methven (nineteen) and Thomas Reid (twenty-three), had left the hut at 10 a.m. to traverse a section of the Cuillin Ridge called the Dubhs. John Roycroft was married with a family and was a research worker at Glasgow University. As well as being an experienced mountaineer he was also a very careful climber. John Methven was unmarried and had a certain amount of climbing experience on both rock and ice. Thomas Reid worked in the university library and he too had some experience of snow and ice climbing. Like John Methven, he was unmarried.

Even before George had finished his soup, I had the main details from him and telephoned the police station in Portree. I told them of the accident and that Catherine, George and I would go up right away, taking with us a tent and a sleeping bag, to try and save the survivor, Methven. I added that the accident had occurred in An Garbh-choire, over the ridge from Coir' a' Ghrunnda, and suggested that their rescue team should go right up into Coir' a' Ghrunnda and cross the ridge to the east side of it, following up the large boulder-field slope. It was then 3.20 p.m.

'In case there is any difficulty,' I added, thinking that it might be very icy on the main ridge, 'one of us will, if possible, shine a torch, either from the crest of the ridge or from where the bodies are. If we're unable to do this, I'll try to get some word to you.'

'That's understood. We'll get some chaps down as soon as possible.'

This rescue was in the days before walkie-talkies were available for mountain-rescue work; if we had had a set with us that night, considerable trouble and misunderstanding would have been avoided.

Invariably, when in climbing areas, I make a point of carrying my rescue equipment with me in the car; I quickly packed this in my climbing sack with some first-aid. Catherine had further first aid and a sleeping bag, while I gave George the lightweight tent that I had with me. We also took a plentiful supply of torch batteries and I gave George new ones for his headlight.

We were just leaving the house, at 4.30 p.m., when I remembered that the Junior Mountaineering Club of Scotland was that day having a meet at Kintail, where the proprietor, Norman Tennant, was acting as host. I said to John Campbell as I went out, 'John, can you give the police another ring and tell them that the JMCS are in Kintail at Kintail Lodge Hotel and, if they telephone Norman Tennant, they might come up?'

'Yes, I'll do that right away. Norman and the club could be quite a help on this.'

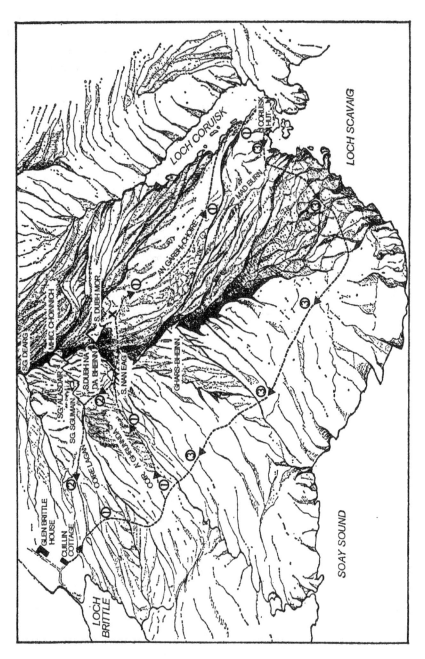

Skye: New Year 1963: the routes taken by the various parties. **1** indicates the route taken by the author's party to X, the place where the bodies were found, and the subsequent route to Coruisk Hut, which was also the route used for the final evacuation. **2** shows the return route of Tennant's party, which took the same approach route to Coir' a-Ghrunnda. **3** marks the path taken by the party which went to Glen Brittle.

'Cheerio,' we called to Mrs Campbell, who was in the kitchen.

'Cheerio, and take care.'

We made fast time up the path which skirts round the side of Sgùrr Dearg and presently we were crossing the open ground across the south of Coire Làgan, where, on the steep face of Sròn na Ciche, we could just pick out in the fading light the icy outline of the Cioch (the Breast), that great protuberance of gabbro, discovered and climbed by the late Professor Norman Collie. Up to our left we could see Sgùrr Alasdair in the greyish light; at 3,257 feet it is the highest peak on Skye. Seen from Glen Brittle, near the beach, and also from the path on which we trod, it forms a huge pyramid high above upper Coire Lagan. It derives its name from Sheriff Alexander Nicholson, a great lover of Skye and a man of the mountains.

By the time we entered Coir' a' Ghrunnda we could see very little. Our breath condensed in front of us, for the temperature was rapidly dropping. We stopped to put on our headlamps and crampons; there were some difficulties ahead. George hadn't come down this way, but had traversed the corrie higher up to descend by the Sgumain Stone Shoot which runs down the side of the face of Sròn na Ciche. This, I felt, would be a slightly quicker way up.

Coir' a' Ghrunnda is in two tiers and rock climbs can be done at both levels in summer. Now, in the grim light of dusk, the smooth ice-worn gabbro glinted with its covering of new ice. The path follows the true right-hand side of the corrie; up this we climbed, our headlights stabbing the gloom. Presently we came to an impasse in the form of an ice wall. The track at this point (if boot-worn boulders deserve such a title) involves a short rock scramble in summer; now it was a smooth sheet of moderately steep ice.

Using my ice axe, I cut huge bucket steps up this, but because of the brittle nature of the ice some of these flaked off when I stood on them. Though there was no real danger, it would, I realised, cause some trouble for the Portree Rescue Team, many of whom had never climbed in winter before. Anyhow, there was nothing that we could do about it and we had to press on, for over the ridge above us there was, we believed, a dying man.

It was 6 p.m. before we reached the level floor of the corrie. This corrie, like many of the Cuillin corries, contains a lochan. At 2,300 feet, Loch Coir' a' Ghrunnda is the highest in the Cuillins.

Silhouetted in starlight, only 300 feet above us, was the crest of the ridge. 'Over it lie two dead and one badly injured climber,' I told myself, and reluctantly carried on without stopping. George was still keeping up with us, though I knew that he must now be feeling very tired.

'How are you, George?' I asked, as we stumbled up through the snow and ice-covered boulders.

'Managing,' he replied tersely. 'Not far to go now.'

As we crested the ridge we were assaulted by a searing easterly wind, the coldest wind experienced in Scotland. It cut at us like a thousand needle points blowing up from the corrie below.

'Where now, George?' I shouted above the wind when he arrived alongside.

'Down on the left somewhere,' he replied. 'There's a big kind of boulder corridor; they are up to the left of that.'

'Hello, Colin!' he shouted, with surprising strength in his voice. Even the wind seemed to hold its breath for a minute as the plaintive call echoed back from the crags mockingly. 'Hello, Colin!'

'Would he hear you from here?' I asked.

'He should do. I don't understand it.'

'Let's go down then. If he has his anorak hood up he won't hear us.'

The three of us picked our way down the steep iced scree. Had we fallen, we should not have gone far, for there were too many jagged boulders embedded in the slope to allow that.

'They must be about here somewhere; we may even have come too far down.'

'Let's spread out and search,' I suggested. Presently, all three of us started to work up and across the steep, broken face of the side of the two peaks – Sgùrr Dubh an Da Bheinn and Sgùrr Dubh Mor – which are close together. Sgùrr Dubh Mòr forms an offshoot from the main ridge to the east where it extends in a narrow neck of rock from Sgùrr Dubh an Da Bheinn, which is on the main ridge and rises above Coir' a' Ghrunnda. In summer the traverse of the Dubhs is a popular excursion; people come round by boat from Glen Brittle and traverse the peaks on their return.

I remember vividly that, while I was searching among those rugged icy boulders this cold winter's night, a poem came to mind that I had read in a Scottish Mountaineering Club journal:

> Said Maylard to Solly one day in Glen Brittle,
> All serious climbing, I vote is a bore:
> Just for once I Dubh Beag you'll agree to do little
> And, as less we can't do, let's go straight to Dubh Mor.
>
> So now when they seek but a day's relaxation,
> With no thought in the world but of viewing the views,
> And regarding the mountains in mute adoration,
> They call it not 'climbing' but 'doing the Dubhs'.

It was uncanny searching that steep mountainside. We strained our ears, half expecting to hear a faint call, but there was nothing. Just the occasional sough of the wind as it would spring up for a second or two, then subside, for we were mostly sheltered from it now.

'Let's have a talk about this,' I shouted to the others.

'Right,' replied George, who was beyond Catherine. 'What do you think?' he asked as he came across, his crampons rasping on the ice.

'I think we're wasting our time. We've searched for more than an hour without success. Let's face it; if Colin was here we would have got a reply from him. He couldn't have come to any harm on his own at this spot.' My head-lamp swept round like a miniature lighthouse beam, forming grotesque shadows amongst the gabbro boulders. 'It's fairly straightforward and he's a competent chap. Either John Methven recovered enough for him to accompany Colin back to the hut, possibly with Cammy and Alan Laird, or John died after you left and Colin decided to go back to the hut on his own.'

'Yes,' said George quietly. 'Either way, we would be better going to Coruisk.'

Even this, I realised, wasn't a satisfactory decision, for I had told the Portree police that we would try and give a signal to the Portree team when they came up into Coir' a' Ghrunnda, but I told myself that since they knew the accident had occurred over the ridge they would be bound to come over, although the difficulties were considerable for an inexperienced party. On the other hand – I reasoned with myself – if I stayed up there and waited for them, it would mean that both Catherine and George would have to go down to the hut on their own and I knew that George was very tired and might have considerable difficulty in finding the way down; the logical course of action was for us all to descend to the hut. From there I would send off two men to intercept the Portree party, for I assumed that they would take some time in getting down to Glen Brittle and up the hill. The possibility of returning to Glen Brittle the way we had come was out of the question as we didn't yet know what had happened to John Methven. Besides, it was too cold for Catherine and George to bivouac on the ridge above, for the wind was arctic.

It was a nasty descent down to Loch Coruisk but a welcome light indicated the position of the hut. We were all tired and George, I felt sure, must have been on his last legs. Above the rush of the water from the Coruisk River we could hear the beat of surf on the shore and, somewhere to the south on one of the islands, the light of a navigational beacon could be seen. I was apprehensive as to what we would find at the hut. Would Methven be there? I told myself that it was most unlikely but one always cherishes a faint glimmer of hope.

At two minutes to midnight we opened the door. I stood aside at the entrance to let George in first.

The hut was filled with GUMC members; several in the party were girls. From Colin Stead we learned that John Methven had died a short time after George had left for Glen Brittle. Cammy and Alan Laird had joined him and they had seen no point in staying with the bodies so had returned to the hut.

What had happened to the climbers is best described by Colin Stead, who was with George and Robert Russell in the search party:

The three lads left the hut at 10 a.m. They were well equipped with reasonable clothing and had torches, but not headlamps. They also had an ice axe apiece and a rope, but no bivouac equipment, for they told us that they would probably be back about 6 p.m. that night. John Methven had no crampons and all three had cleated rubber-soled boots.

The party did not return as expected and, as the evening wore on, we became more uneasy. The customary Hogmanay celebrations did not take place. It was a superb night, clear and windless; down at the hut it was freezing. A lookout was kept for our three friends and a party went up to the head of Loch Coruisk, but saw nothing.

Next morning everyone was up early and a search party was organised. There were fourteen people in the hut, seven of whom were girls. Of the fourteen, Clammy McLeay (not a member of the club) was the senior and most experienced person present. George Wallace and myself were also experienced winter climbers. Two others, Robert Russell and Alan Laird, were rock climbers with limited winter experience. The remainder of the party were largely hill walkers.

It was decided that McLeay and Laird would form a climbing team to follow the route taken by the missing men. Meanwhile, Wallace, Russell and myself would gain the main Cuillin Ridge at the head of Coir' a' Ghrunnda and work in the opposite direction until we met up with them. In this manner it was hoped to cover all the likely ground. The remaining people were to search the corries on either side of the Dubh Ridge and any ground not requiring actual climbing.

By 9 a.m. the search was under way. I think that, by this time, we all expected the missing men to appear – we could hardly think that anything serious might have happened – though Cammy told me later that he had feared the worst.

As our party set off some light snow was falling, but this soon cleared and it turned into an incredibly beautiful day, crisp and sunny with little or no wind. Above 2,000 feet there was a good covering of iron-hard snow, in short, conditions were absolutely perfect.

We gained the main ridge south of the Thearlaich Dubh Gap (an awkward step on the main ridge) from Coir' an Lochain. We were, of course, shouting and searching all the time. I remember little of time or distance. At one point we saw McLeay and Laird away in the distance and a shouted conversation took place which we completely misinterpreted, taking it to mean that the missing men had been found safe. (At this time we were somewhere on the Dubh Ridge; I had never been on this part of the Cuillins before and my knowledge of it was scanty.)

Soon we came across a reasonably angled snow gully which appeared to lead down into An Garbh-choire and we decided to investigate it. We were then happy in the belief that our friends were safe. A short distance down the gully we found an ice axe which belonged to Tom Reid. It was just lying on the surface of the snow. Here, too, we found signs of crampon marks, the first we had seen. There were unmistakable indications that a slide had occurred. A hundred feet lower we found gloves and some blood. The snow was very hard and the gully was now a bit steeper. We descended unroped, kicking in the front points of our crampons and facing the slope, the picks of our ice axes driven in above us, as we progressed downwards. Some 400 feet lower we found our missing friends. They were lying on a step in the gully, below which it dropped sharply in some ice pitches. Ironically, there was an easy way down to the floor of the corrie on the left side of the gully.

Tom was dead, sitting with his back against the step, his arms folded across his chest. His crampons had been wrenched off in the fall. John was lying face down on the floor of the step. He, too, was dead. John Methven was sitting on the edge of the step; they were still roped together. George reached them first. John Methven seemed unconscious, moving his head slightly and mumbling incoherently. Both he and John Roycroft still had their axes attached to their wrists by their slings, but John Roycroft had lost his crampons on the fall. We did what little we could for John but were afraid to move him.

As George had the greatest knowledge of the Cuillins we decided he should get across to Glen Brittle as quickly as possible for assistance. Russell descended to collect extra blankets from the hut. I stayed with John Methven. It was then about 2 p.m. Fifteen minutes later John died quietly, without regaining consciousness.

I remember that time vividly; I sat shattered and lonely. It was my first experience with death. I decided to wait for Cammy McLeay and Alan Laird; when I heard them above me, I blew my whistle and they came down. Cammy verified that all three were dead.

They [Cammy and Colin] had done the round trip of the Dubh Ridge to 'death gully' in four or five hours. They hadn't used a rope but Cammy said that the three dead men had done so, for they had seen marks of it, here and there, in softer patches of snow. John Methven's lack of crampons must have been a serious handicap in the hard conditions which prevailed; this was probably why they had remained roped up the whole way.

We reckoned then that they must have reached the top of the gully after dark and, from our own experience, it did look a temptingly easy way down the gully. Finally, we decided that it would be best for us to go back to the hut and inform the others that John Methven, too, was dead …

There was a strange atmosphere in the crowded hut. You could feel the tension in the air, hanging like a heavy cloud. Some of the party simply sat and stared; others were listless; anyone who spoke was intensely aware of a silent and unresponsive audience. One of the girls, however, had the presence of mind to make us some tea and something to eat.

I said to Cammy, the only one I knew at all in the group, 'Someone will have to go round to Glen Brittle right away to advise the other rescue groups of the situation. Otherwise they'll be searching the Cuillins all night.'

'Any volunteers?' I asked the assembled group. 'It will have to be two people who are both fit and know the path reasonably well.'

'I think that Cammy and myself are the only two who fill that bill,' said Colin. 'We'll go.'

'You must be pretty tired,' I ventured doubtfully. 'Do you know the path?'

'No, I don't. Do you, Cammy?'

'I was along part of it once – but can't you tell us where it goes?'

'Well, I can,' I said. 'But it's not easy to find, even in daylight. If you two do that, George and I can go up at first light and start taking the bodies down. I understand that they are in quite a difficult position.'

'We'd better start right away, then,' said Cammy. 'At least we've had a few hours' rest.'

'Tell the police that a boat will be the best way to evacuate the bodies. With the help of the others we can take the bodies down to the jetty.'

'Righto.'

They set off as soon as they were equipped with new batteries for their head-lamps. I had described as carefully as possible where the path went but I knew that they were bound to lose it, for it was extremely difficult to follow.

Despite this difficulty, and the darkness, Cammy and Colin took less than four and a half hours to reach McRae's barn in Glen Brittle, arriving at 4.55 a.m., just as the RAF team was about to set off. They met nobody on the way.

But, to go back in time a little: at my suggestion, the Portree police had telephoned Kintail Lodge Hotel after they had alerted the RAF Mountain

Rescue Team, who were spending New Year at Cameron's barn, Glen Nevis; the team had promised to leave as quickly as possible.

Already they had had their share of trouble, for they had been on a call-out for two climbers who had fallen in Green Gully on Ben Nevis and they had also been down to assist at the tail end of a rescue in Glencoe, just before I left the glen, and had stayed the night in my barn. Next, on 29 December, they had travelled up to Kinlochewe overnight, on a call-out; the journey took five hours from Fort William on exceptionally icy roads. The team felt they had earned their keep as they returned to Fort William to start the New Year festivities. They looked forward to a peaceful and blissful few days but, even before Hogmanay, a further accident took place – one of their own chaps fell while going up the iced path to Ben Nevis.

John Hinde was then the flight-sergeant in charge of the team. He had recently returned from an expedition in Alaska where he had his toes frostbitten. Despite this handicap he was still getting about, though not back to his usual active self. John is a tall, quiet-spoken man and the fact that he is liked and respected by everyone in the rescue team is a high recommendation, for their assessment of fellow team members, and especially their team leader, is stringently critical.

While he was in the Fort William hospital, visiting McLeod who had broken his leg on the icy Ben Nevis path, he received a message to say that there was a call-out in the Cuillins. How he managed to gather up his flock that New Year's Day remains a miracle. They were scattered to the four winds. Many were still sleeping it off in the houses of friends, as far apart as Kinlochleven and Spean Bridge, while in Fort William some parties were still going strong.

The road to the isles has been much improved since that time; then, much of the way was single track and there were many short, steep hills which were particularly subject to icing. It was 6 p.m. by the time the RAF trucks passed through Kintail.

Shortly before, Norman Tennant had received the call for assistance from the Portree police. The club had just assembled in the dining room to partake of the superb dinner that Norman had prepared. Norman, as well as being a mountaineer of great experience, is a culinary wizard. A delectable entrée had been eagerly devoured by the hungry guests, who had spent a hard day on the hills and were looking forward with enthusiasm to the main dish – turkey – which was just being brought in by the waitresses.

Norman, who is so quiet-spoken that on occasions it can be difficult to hear what he's saying, returned from the telephone and announced quite casually, 'I'm afraid, chaps, that there's been an accident in the Cuillins; we've been asked to go and help.'

There was a sudden pause in the drone of conversation and a frenzied scramble as the club members, galvanised into action, grabbed at turkey legs, or whatever fare was to hand, and rushed to their respective rooms for their climbing gear.

An assortment of cars left Kintail Lodge Hotel that evening. Jim Simpson, Kenny Brian and Roger Robb were in Norman's Cooper S. Norman rejoiced in a certain notoriety for driving hotted-up cars and this was, in some respects, well earned. In a short period of time he wrote off two Coopers, miraculously escaping serious injury. As a matter of fact, after his second crash I suggested he should start up a Cooper S taxi service in Paris and I am sure that he gave this proposal second thoughts.

By the time the cars of the JMCS were climbing the long, steep hill on the old road over to Dornie, the RAF trucks were descending to the village. The steep hill was icy and there was little sand on it. Norman and the rest of the JMCS party drew in behind the trucks at Kyle of Lochalsh. The police had forewarned the ferry authorities that a special ferry would be required to take the rescuers across to Skye, and it was just coming into the jetty as Norman's party drew to a halt.

As they were carefully nosing the cars and trucks aboard, an old car skidded down the ramp and tried to get aboard. Gerry Pete, recognising the occupant as the proprietor and sole reporter of a freelance news agency – rejoicing in the name of 'Scoop' – gave a shout for reinforcements and persuaded the driver that there was no room on the ferry and that in any case it was a special charter trip.

Past Sligachan, on Skye, the road climbs a hill and then goes along a straight before it reaches Carbost, the home of that famous and quite delectable malt whisky – Talisker. Here Norman, possibly encouraged by the first stretch of straight road since leaving Kintail, put his foot down. His action unfortunately coincided with a particularly vicious sheet of black ice, difficult to detect in the headlights. The car spun round and round again, still remaining, miraculously, upon the road. It was stated, at a later date, that at this moment Kenny Brian opened an eye. Whether this was in awakening or in fright, or both, was never clarified. The car was manhandled round to face the right direction again and they continued with undiminished speed.

At 10.40 p.m. Norman's party arrived at Glen Brittle House, where they were met by a police sergeant, Murdo James McLeod, from Portree. He seemed to be in a most cheerful mood!

'Where is the accident?' asked Kenny, unfolding himself from the car.

'It's in one of those corries at the back of Sgùrr Alasdair ... let's see... yes, it begins with 'G' ... '

'Coir' a' Ghrunnda,' prompted Norman hopefully.

'Yes, that's it,' replied the sergeant, beaming. 'Och, you'll have no trouble; the Portree boys are away up and you'll see them in the corrie.'

Wasting no time, the party set off, and they were only a short way up the hill when the first RAF vehicle came down the glen, its headlights picking out Highland cattle lying asleep on the frozen grass. The RAF arrived at McRae's barn at 11 p.m. and started to unload their gear.

The Portree police team had left some hours previously. They also had a hard time in finding all their members. This team is made up with both civilian and police members, under the leadership of John MacKenzie from the post office in Portree. That night PC Kenny MacKenzie was with them; Kenny was later to be posted to Kinlochleven, where he played a major part in the rescues on Ben Nevis and in Glencoe. Others in the party were PC Roy MacKenzie, PC Norman McLeod, George Bell, who was a gamekeeper on Skye, Johnny MacInnes, who worked in Portree, and Willie Sutherland, who, as well as being the Glen Brittle Hostel Warden, ran the local bus service. Kenny McKinnon, a TA sergeant in Portree, Neill Drummond and two other policemen made up the official party. They took with them an old Thomas stretcher and one pressure lamp, which was being carried by the son of Lord Malcolm Douglas Hamilton. Lord Malcolm, as he was known to many on Skye, was at one time the MP for Inverness-shire and had done much climbing in the Cuillins; tragically, both he and his son later died in a plane crash in Africa. There was one other in the group, a friend of young Douglas Hamilton – Andrew Roberts, who professed some climbing knowledge.

This group came to an abrupt halt at the bottom of the steep ice wall on which I had cut steps, for they had no crampons although most of them had ice axes. John MacKenzie, who had some experience on snow and ice, took up the lead then, climbed the pitch and fixed a rope to a rock bollard at the top; up this the group scrambled, their nailed boots scraping against the hard ice. Two members of the party decided to stay below as they were feeling tired and the ice pitch looked too much for them.

'Well, you both stay there until we come back down again,' shouted John MacKenzie. 'We don't want to have too many people wandering about the mountain.'

Some way above this point John MacKenzie, Kenny McKinnon and Neill Drummond went on ahead, asking Kenny, Roy and Johnny MacInnes, with the two young climbers, to remain there with the stretcher – they would shout down if it was required. Johnny and Kenny, who were holding the stretcher shafts, thankfully swung it across the snow slope, jammed it behind a boulder and sat on it. The pressure lamp cast a bright circle of light around them as they huddled there, tired and cold.

Once the top party had reached the corrie beside the lochan, they realised that they would be unable to climb over the ridge that night. They found it, as I did, hard and treacherous. It was too steep and dangerous for them in the dark. Besides, none of them had suitable equipment so it would have been foolhardy for them to attempt it. There was nothing they could do but to go back down. There was no sign of the signal which I had arranged so they realised that something must have occurred to interfere with the plan. They retraced their steps back to the stretcher party.

'Have any luck?' asked Roy, as the three men came down to the rocks.

'Can't see a thing,' said John. 'It's as dark as the Earl of Hell's waistcoat up there and there's not a light to be seen.'

'I suppose we'd better go back down then,' rejoined Kenny, unwrapping a sweet.

'There may be some word now at the farm.'

'Aye, let's get moving,' someone else muttered. 'Or we'll freeze to death. Hamish's party must have gone down to Coruisk, I suppose.'

They began the descent to the ice pitch where the rope had been left. At a steep, rocky pitch young Douglas Hamilton, who had been holding the lantern to illuminate the descent for those with the stretcher, slipped and fell on to the party below, just missing the stretcher, breaking the pressure lamp and grazing the cheek of John MacInnes. As he gathered himself up, brushing off snow, someone was heard to remark, 'Another few feet to the right and he would have been on the stretcher; that would have been service!'

The drama for the night was not yet finished. There was now only one good torch left and that belonged to Kenny MacKenzie. When they reached the ice pitch they descended it, one at a time. Andrew was the last to descend, after which they discovered that the doubled rope had frozen to the rock bollard above. Since he was the only self-professed ice climber in the group, the task fell to him to climb back up and free it. He managed this after some effort but it still refused to free from below. His only alternative was either to leave the rope there or to climb down without it; he took the latter course, using some artificial aids.

Kenny MacKenzie is a good six feet tall and built like a rock gendarme. George Bell climbed on to his shoulders and, balancing thereon with an ugly nailed boot each side of Kenny's head, straightened up slowly and leant against the ice. He then reached up with his hands to his full extent and just managed to touch the soles of the boots of Andrew who was, at this time, in danger of falling. With an ungainly motion the human pyramid retracted, and those who watched by the dim light of their headlamps swore that Kenny's legs buckled under the strain. At last they all gasped with relief as the pyramid collapsed in a heap at the bottom of the ice.

Norman Tennant had by this time crossed the mouth of Coire Làgan with his small team of climbers. They arrived at the bottom of the ice pitch just as the human pyramid act had finished, thereby missing what must have been one of the most unusual exhibitions of combined tactics in the history of Scottish mountaineering.

'Good evening,' said Norman in his usual quiet manner, as if he had perhaps met a number of colleagues in Sauchiehall Street. 'Have you seen anything of Hamish's group?'

'Not a thing,' said John. 'There isn't a sign of anything up above and there's a hell of a lot of ice leading up to the ridge.'

'Well, I suppose, seeing we are here,' interjected Kenny Brian, sitting down on a rock and sorting out his crampons, 'we may as well go up and have a look.'

'Anyone got any light?' asked Jimmy Simpson, trying to undo the straps that held his crampons on to his rucksack.

'Aye, there's a switch on the wall beside you,' retorted Johnny MacInnes, which seemed so funny to the assembled group that they all doubled up in laughter.

Five minutes later they all had their crampons on and, after stamping them into the ice at the bottom of the pitch to get the feel of them, they started up. By the time they had reached the top, the Portree team had started down again with the stretcher and very little light to guide them. From the top Norman's voice floated down to them, 'Be seeing you.'

However, they had no more success in finding the scene of the accident than ourselves; after taking a high line round the corrie, they cut across to the top of the Sgumain Stone Shoot, where George Wallace had first descended to Glen Brittle. About an hour later, the Portree team saw the lights of Norman's party descending the Stone Shoot *en route* for Glen Brittle. For some reason Cammy and Colin, who had travelled round from Coruisk, didn't see them at all and the groups arrived at the farm independently at half-hour intervals.

At McRae's barn the RAF and the JMCS were having an early breakfast, prior to setting off. They were still awaiting some definite news before taking action, but by 4 a.m. they decided to have something to eat and were preparing to leave at 5 a.m. As they went outside Cammy and Colin arrived.

'They're all dead,' said Colin to John Hinde as they approached.

'Come on inside,' John suggested, 'and have a brew.'

Once they were settled on some bales of hay they told their story, saying that Catherine, George and I had arrived at the hut at midnight after failing to locate the bodies.

'Well, there doesn't seem to be any great urgency now,' said John, and went to have a word with Murdo James.

They concluded that the best scheme now would be to obtain a boat, as I had suggested, so that everyone could be ferried round and the bodies evacuated. Murdo went off to telephone police headquarters in Portree from the call box outside the barn. Presently he returned and told John that the *Western Isles* was being chartered by the police and they hoped to have it in Loch Brittle by midday.

'Well, that's a relief,' said John thankfully. 'It'll save a long hike.'

'Okay, chaps,' he shouted. 'You can get back to bed. A late breakfast at ten o'clock, Cook, please.'

'Oh, no, not another one,' moaned the cook good-naturedly. Most of the lads went straight to sleep in their clothes and slept the sleep of the just until ten.

The *Western Isles* is a stout, clinker-built boat owned by the skipper, Brucy Watt. His base is at Mallaig and he uses the craft for a passenger service to the islands of Rùm, Eigg and Muck, besides running summer cruises round the Western Isles after which she is appropriately named. It wasn't until 11.30 a.m. that she was sighted, turning the headland at Rubha an Dùnain. One 3-ton truck was already bogged down on the beach so the services of Gidean McRae, the farmer's son, had to be enlisted to extricate the vehicle with his tractor. As there is no jetty at Loch Brittle it took a considerable time to ferry all the party out to the boat; there was a total of twenty-five men, ten of them civilians.

John Hinde told George Paterson to take one of the three-ton trucks round to either Elgol or Broadford, for he didn't know then where the bodies would be taken by the boat.

'The police will advise you as to where the boat is going, George,' he called as he jumped into the dinghy.

'Aye, right you are,' shouted George in his broad Aberdonian accent. 'I'll give them a ring. Good luck, lads.'

It was 2 p.m. before the boat berthed at the natural rock jetty at Coruisk. The journey had been uneventful; just cold and bleak.

Meanwhile, we had had a restless night in the hut, despite being tired. I was awakened several times by girls sobbing; someone else had a nightmare and the loud screams woke everyone up. Dawn seems reluctant to come in these northern latitudes but the grey light had filtered through the windows before anyone got up. Despite the fact we were at sea level, there was a keen frost outside and a terrible fug within the hut. One of the girls asked if we would like breakfast.

'Yes, please. I suppose we'd better make a move. Can you come back up with me this morning, George?' I turned towards him.

'Aye, I'll do that. Perhaps a couple of the other lads here can come as well.'

'We should be able to take the bodies down a little way, George; otherwise we're going to get caught in darkness again.'

Catherine had decided to return to Glen Brittle via the shore path so we said 'cheerio' to her as we set off again up the side of Loch Coruisk. We made good time that crisp morning. Though the weather wasn't fine, at least it wasn't snowing, but to the south and west we could see a deep bank of cloud which I knew usually presaged bad weather in the Hebrides. Leading up into An Garbh-choire from the shores of Coruisk are long boilerplate slabs which make the ascent both interesting and easy. But, from time to time, large boulder fields had to be negotiated which I knew would hamper the evacuation later in the day.

Even with George's assistance, we had trouble in locating the bodies. They were grouped close together, within ten feet of each other. Their equipment was scattered over the gully bed above, some if it embedded in the hard, frozen snow. Roycroft was tied at one end of the rope; as he was the most experienced we assumed that he had been descending last, the accepted technique on descent. John Methven, who was the least experienced and had no crampons, was tied to the other end of the rope. George indicated the point from which he thought they had fallen; this, as accurately as we could estimate, was about 400 feet above.

One of the club members who had come up with us felt so ill at the sight of his dead friends that he had to go away.

'We were just over there last night, George.' I pointed to some large boulders, sticking out of the clear ice like small, dark icebergs.

'It can't be more than 100 feet away,' he replied.

We cut the rope from the bodies to use as a kind of rope stretcher. First, however, we used it to lower one body down a short, steep rock cliff; I went down an easier and more indirect way to collect it at the bottom. George and the other club climber joined me about ten minutes later.

'Look,' exclaimed George. 'Down below, there's a party coming up.'

'So there is. It must be some of the boat party.' We hadn't realised that it had come in and, as a matter of fact, were wondering if it would ever materialise.

As the party drew nearer, I recognised most of the rescuers. In the front was Cammy McLeay, followed by Spike, Jack Baines and Ned Calligan of the RAF team.

'Hello there,' I called. 'We're glad to see you chaps; we thought we might have to take these three down on our own.'

'Sorry we're late, Hamish. The boat didn't come in until about midday.'

'Quite a mess,' said Jack, when we had taken them up to the bodies.

'That's some pace you set up,' muttered Ned as he drew alongside Cammy.

'Are the others on their way?' I asked.

'Yes, but they're a bit behind.'

'What about sending up a flare?' suggested Jack. 'We did say that we would give them a signal when we reached you. None of the party down there' – he stabbed with his ice axe in the direction of the lower corrie – 'know exactly where we are.'

'They'll have to be blind not to see that,' said Spike, looking up as the rocket shot up 600 feet and exploded in a red plume. Unfortunately, as soon as it was fired we realised that it might actually be confusing for, though the flare was conspicuous enough, the point from which it was fired might have been located anywhere within a radius of over 800 feet. As a result, the support party took the wrong approach into the corrie and went too high. This delayed their arrival by about half an hour. They were a large group, some twenty-five members, including the JMCS men with Gerry Pete. Norman's party were still sleeping it off after their overnight sortie, but John MacKenzie and some of the Portree chaps were back up after a sleepless and active night.

We went back to the foot of the rock cliff and started once more. First we had to lower the body down a snow slope on the rope; then we used two ice axes, at right angles across the body, with short lengths of rope tied to the wrists and ankles. Gerry Pete remarked afterwards, 'It was a macabre sight – four men carrying the body hanging from ice axes'.

Meanwhile, Jack, Spike and the others had made two similar rope stretchers and were now moving down with the other bodies.

Chiefy Hinde was in the van of the support team.

'Good afternoon, John. Keeping office hours these days?'

'Hi, Hamish; the transport services are a bit sluggish in these parts. It looks as if we have a problem,' he added, as we put the body down beside him. Behind him the party was strung out – like a line of Himalayan porters – some still a long way back.

'Pity about that flare,' I said. 'None of us realised that it might cause confusion.'

'I think the wind must have caused it to drift a bit,' he mused. 'There's certainly not a great deal of wind here, but up there it's stirring a bit.' He looked up to the main ridge.

'What's the forecast?'

'Force eight.'

'Ah well,' I sighed, resigned to this run of bad luck. 'How many are in your party, John?'

'Thirty, including Jack's group above.'

'Then I'll take ten men and start down with this chap.' I pointed to the body at our feet.

'That's probably the best idea,' he agreed. 'You will know the easiest route to take.'

'Is there one?' I asked. 'It's all pretty bloody: slabs, ice and boulders.'

Our task was to take three bodies down 2,300 feet over some of the most difficult terrain in the country. It was 3.40 p.m. and would be dark in about an hour. We strapped the body to the old Thomas stretcher, attached two rear ropes to it, and set off. I tried to keep it moving just as quickly as possible for I knew that the higher up that slope we were when caught by darkness, the more difficult it would be.

All thirty-five of us on that evacuation found it a living hell. It was bitterly cold and boulders kept being knocked down by the others above us. The stretchers, when they were not actually jamming between boulders, kept threatening to become uncontrollable on the long, steep sections of ice which offered no friction whatsoever. Our crampons bit into the ice which frequently broke off in slabs, like sheets of broken glass, so that for an instant – just holding on to the stretcher – we would be out of control until our crampons bit again into the glacier-worn slab beneath.

Some lights appeared from below; we were then at the 1,500 feet contour. It was Colin Stead with Kenny MacKenzie, Roy MacKenzie and Nev Collingham – Nev was from the RAF team and was suffering from a minor leg injury.

It was dark long before my party reached the valley floor. The dark shimmering water of Loch Coruisk looked like a dirty mirror and now clouds were scudding over the Cuillins. It seemed to me as if we were actors in a drama in this great natural amphitheatre; the black Cuillins forming a sombre backcloth and the title role played by Death.

John Hinde had charge of the next body and was only a short way behind. Now, on a very wide slabby section, it was possible for him to take a slightly different line of descent so that, for a time, we didn't have the additional hazard of falling rocks. Jock and Spike, with some of the JMSC boys, had the worst time. They had least light for getting down the difficult section and their stretcher kept sticking. For some reason their body was strapped head first on to the stretcher. This made little difference until, descending a steep iced chimney, the stretcher stuck. Then the head end being heavier made it more difficult for Jack, who was guiding it down, to free it. He was, by this time, thirty feet down the steep chimney; to maintain his position there it was necessary both to hold on to the stretcher and to stamp his crampons vigorously into the ice to obtain a grip with his feet. In his own words, this is how Jack recollects the situation:

> The wooden runners of the stretcher were jammed tight between two faces of gabbro. There was so much friction with the rock that I couldn't pull the runners out of this vice-like gap. I asked the others above to slacken off a bit on the ropes and got between the two lower shafts; leaning back at right angles to the iced rock, I heaved and heaved. Suddenly, the bloody thing freed and I shot down, still holding on to the shafts. I didn't go far, however, for there wasn't that much slack and the stretcher was arrested by the ropes with a sickening jerk. My headlight was shining up the parallel lines of the two top ropes. Though the stretcher stopped, the deceased passenger didn't – and shot out of his securing straps to hit me, head first, in the face. I shit bricks, I really did; I thought he had come to life, but I held him and we were lowered, in ungainly fashion, to easier ground below.

By the time we had the bodies down at the fringe of the loch, our torches were almost finished. We staggered and cursed our way along the loch-side path – if it can be called a path – and were first to arrive back at the hut. It was probably one of the most exacting rescues that any of us had been on; every joint and muscle in our bodies protested, but we were still not finished for we had to get back to either Elgol or Armadale in the boat. The wind, as predicted, was rising; there were indications of a nasty night ahead, though it wasn't yet raining.

At the hut I met John Wilkinson, a tall, active climber with whom I had done several routes in the past.

'Hi, Wilkie,' I greeted him, as I recognised him in the light from the doorway.

'How do you do, Hamish. Sorry I couldn't be of much use, but I've buggered my knee and can hardly walk.'

'You're lucky,' I rejoined, sitting down, exhausted, on the stretcher beside the body. 'It's been a grim trip.'

A pale, slim girl, who had been cheerful up till then, came out of the hut; she took one look at the frozen, covered corpse and fainted.

'The party in the hut are a bundle of nerves,' he jerked his head, indicating the hut occupants, and reached down to pick the girl up.

'Aye, they were last night.'

'The girlfriend of one of the boys who was killed is in there,' said Colin. 'Anyhow, let's see if we can organise them into preparing a meal.' We all trooped into the hut.

Murdo James, who had come round in the *Western Isles*, had not been idle. Once the rescue group had been put ashore and the situation established, he got Brucy Watt to take him over the island of Soay, of shark-fishing fame; from there he had contacted police headquarters by radio telephone via Mallaig. He was back before we reached the hut.

The girls had prepared a huge meal from their own supplies and those brought round by the RAF. There was also an abundance of drink, so by the time we left the hut we were feeling much better. We carried the three bodies down to the *Western Isles*, which was bucking slightly, even in the sheltered water of Loch Scavaig. The bodies were lashed on board and as she pulled away we shouted 'cheerio' to Cammy, Colin and George, who came to see us off; they would return to Mallaig later.

We all went down into the fo'c'sle. The lads were in better spirits now after the tension of the descent and rescue, but the strain of the ordeal was stamped on our faces even before the boat hit the first squall as she cleared the island of Soay, which lies to the west of Loch Scavaig. Someone started to sing …

It is a common tendency amongst rescuers to make light of death. Not that anyone feels callous, but there is a natural reaction towards the other extreme

– merriment – which, I think, helps one to weather the grim possibility that it could have been any of us up there on the spray-washed deck. None of us on the boat that night knew any of the three deceased personally, but we were all very much aware of the grief that we knew must ensue for their parents and friends.

The *Western Isles* started to pitch and a new voice, possibly taking this for a cue, rose above the other disjointed and half-hearted snatches of song:

> They built the ship *Titanic* to sail the ocean blue ...

With a great roar, the entire Kinloss Rescue Team joined in the chorus:

> Husbands and wives, little children lost their lives,
> On the day that the great ship went dow-ow-ow-ow-own ...

A bottle of rum appeared and Kenny MacKenzie, who was sitting on my right – thinking that I didn't drink – leant across and grabbed it from my neighbour on the left; I hastily intervened and gulped gratefully at the fiery liquid. The song was growing in tempo now and there were no more solo parts. It felt as if the deckhead would lift; the noise was deafening ...

> The lifeboats they set sail, 'cross the dark and stormy sea,
> And the band struck up with 'Hail My Lord to Thee',
> Husbands and wives ...

The more violent the passage became, the more volume was produced by the crowd in the smoke-filled fo'c'sle that night.

Meanwhile, George Paterson had telephoned the police in Portree, who told him that, in view of the bad weather forecast, the *Western Isles* would sail round the Point of Sleat and put in to Armadale; he should now proceed to that jetty. At 5 p.m. he took the three-tonner up the steep hill at the head of Glen Brittle on the first stage of his journey. The roads were icier than ever and he had trouble getting up round the hairpin bend near the top of this pass. George himself takes up the narrative:

> When I arrived at the pier, everything was in darkness. The piermaster had locked up his office. As I drew the truck to a halt I said to myself, 'This must be the place but why isn't there a light on?' I just sat in the cab, waiting for something to happen. Soon a Dormobile-like van drew up and I went over to where it had stopped, about twenty feet away. It was bitterly cold and I turned my coat collar up. They were two boot-faced chaps

[Pakistanis] and the van was a kind of ambulance, probably just used for bodies on the island. I got talking to them, hoping they might invite me inside where it would be warm, but they were a couple of dour chaps and not very communicative so I went back to my truck. It was about a quarter to eight.

In about half an hour a car drew up – it was some reporters from the *Daily Express*. They were much more friendly and, what's more, they had a half-bottle! We had just finished this, about ten minutes later, when the piermaster came along and put on the lights. I went over and had a word with him to ask him when the boat was due.

'Oh, about a quarter to nine, I've been told.'

'Well, I can't see any sign of it,' I said, and was just going back to the reporters when he said, 'We could go somewhere a wee bit warmer.'

I didn't object when he took us to the pub.

In Skye, you know, they don't use glasses at New Year; they use tumblers. Between us we polished off quite a bit of whisky before half past ten, but there was still no sign of the boat. The publican said to us 'Well, chaps, it's getting late, but don't go away. I'll have to close the doors; I gather that the inspector is on his way down.'

In view of this, we all thought it better to adjourn to one of the policemen's houses – Norman McLeod's.

His house had a grand view of the Sound of Sleat, though it was then dark of course, but any ship coming up the Sound could be spotted immediately. From then on our tumblers weren't allowed to be emptied at all for this would have been a terrible state of affairs in Skye at New Year. Presently the inspector arrived and joined the company. I sang 'The Buchan Bobby'; this went down quite well in police circles! I remember, just a wee while after I had finished the song, I looked at my watch for about the hundredth time that night; it said one o'clock and I said out loud, 'That's five bloody hours I've been waiting and, do you know, I haven't had any sleep for five nights; this is the fifth night.'

'No, I think I've had enough to drink,' I told the piermaster as he was topping up my almost empty tumbler for the tenth time. 'I've got to drive the lads back to Glen Brittle tonight and I must stay sober!'

Somebody beside the window shouted, 'A light, a light … '

It was one of the reporters and the last few syllables were slurred. It was then 1.10 a.m. on 3 January.

> I'll never forget that boat coming in. It was rocking like a mad
> thing and I wondered if this was caused by the gale or the roar-
> ing of a song which reached us on the pier. It was the sixteenth
> verse of the 'Ball of Kirriemuir' – I mind it fine.

As soon as the *Western Isles* had tied alongside we got out of the fo'c'sle and
went ashore. We were struck by the arctic blast of the wind which hit us, for
down below it had been snug and warm. We could see a small group of people
assembled under the naked light of the booking office. George was with them,
swaying slightly, or was it that we were still orientated to the pitch of the boat?

'Hello, George,' Chiefy called. 'Come to drive us home?'

'I've got the truck all ready, John; how many have you got?'

John realised from George's speech that his festivities had been protracted
and said, 'I'd better drive, George. We have more than a full load; some of
them will have to stay here until tomorrow.'

'I'm all right, John, honest; I'm not a bit the worst. I've not drunk anything
but whisky all night.'

'Aye,' said John laughing. 'But how much?'

We all piled into the three-tonner. I squeezed into the cab beside George
who was propped between Chiefy, the driver, and myself. There wasn't room
for everyone so some of the RAF lads elected to stay behind. The piermaster
offered them the use of the waiting room for the remainder of the night.
Even before the truck roared off into the darkness, they were settled into their
sleeping bags on the chilly, concrete floor. Below the floor, under the pier,
lapped the cold water of the Atlantic.

All things considered, they fared better than we did. When they woke in the
morning the steamer was tied up alongside and they were invited aboard for
breakfast. At opening time they adjourned to the pub for a half-pint of beer
apiece. They had calculated that their total wealth would just stretch so far.

'Four half-pints, please,' said Jack as he reached the bar.

'Four half-pints,' repeated the barman, looking at them closely.

'That's right.'

He took the malt whisky bottle off the shelf and poured four large whiskies;
then drew four pints of beer.

'There you are, lads.'

'But,' said Jack, taken aback and rapidly calculating what this would cost,
'we only want four half-pints.'

'You're some of the lads that were on the rescue, are you not?'

'Yes.'

'Well then; it's on me. Drink up.'

Before this round was finished the piermaster came in and ordered another
round. Next, Norman McLeod came in and stood them a round. Then the

minister arrived and did the same. By the time the truck was back to pick them up they realised how George had succumbed to the Skye hospitality!

As we left Armadale the previous night, we were all feeling the reaction from over-strain and lack of sleep. I could see John nodding at the wheel, no doubt lulled by George's sonorous, whisky-laden snores. The roads were desperately bad; there was black ice everywhere. From countless journeys to Skye, I knew the road as well as I knew my own house and I said to John as we were nearing Sconser, 'There's a nasty bridge ahead.'

'What was that?' he said with a start.

'There's a bad bridge coming up,' I yelled as it suddenly loomed up in the headlights.

'Christ,' he shouted, as he wrenched the wheel. 'We'll never make it.' We skidded between the parapets, which weren't much wider than the truck. 'That was close!'

The main road to Portree was then mainly single track; not the wide high-way it is today. However, we reached the approach to Sligachan Hotel without further incident other than the occasional slide, any one of which, had it continued, would have broken through the flimsy wooden railing, the only barrier to the drop on to the rocky beach far below. We seemed to be approaching the old humpback bridge at the hotel rather fast. I didn't like to say anything this time, for I am sure he would have thought I was chicken. We were going too fast, however, and the three-tonner didn't quite make the corner at the bridge – it hit the parapet. These trucks are unusually robust and the damage wasn't severe enough to hinder our progress; John's physical condition was, though! He was exhausted and could no longer keep his eyes open; he drew into the lay-by beside the hotel. George awoke with a start.

'Why don't you let Cookie drive?' asked George when he saw the predicament.

'Aye, may as well,' said John, climbing out.

'I might just as well be driving,' said Bob Cook as he climbed in and John took his place in the rear. 'There's not much hope of a sleep back there; it's like riding on a curling stone!'

Bob drove well and reached the hills between Carbost and the steep descent to Glen Brittle before we ran into trouble again. This time it was ice covering the road on a very steep, short hill. The truck spun to a halt and he had to slew it into the ditch to prevent it sliding back down the hill again and perhaps going off the road at the bottom where there was a narrow wooden bridge. I jumped out and Spike climbed down from the rear with a couple of ice axes.

'Let's cut the ice under the wheels; then make grooves across the road in the ice, so that she can get a grip,' he said.

'Good idea. Give me an axe, then.'

For about ten minutes we hacked away and presently Cookie, who had turned off the engine, came to join us.

'That should help,' he observed, shining his torch on the glistening road. 'It's like a bloody skating rink.'

We were just in front of the truck now, having completed about thirty feet of furrowing from the rear wheels, when George, aroused once more from his slumberings by the unnatural silence, jumped across into the driver's seat and started up. The truck roared behind us as he banged it into gear; the four wheels bit into the grooves in the ice and it shot up the hill. Bob had just enough time to jump on to the running board as it passed, but Spike and I were left in the middle of the road, shouting abuses at George in long and varied strings and waving our ice axes. The rear lights receded into the distance, leaving us together on that lonely moor.

George swears now that he knew we were back there, but didn't dare stop in case they couldn't get going again. There may be some truth in this claim, for we came across the truck again, about a mile farther on at the top of the rise, and proceeded without incident to Glen Brittle, eventually arriving at 4 a.m.

Since New Year's Day, 1963, I have always made a point of heading for the city or a seaside resort if I want to go somewhere quiet for a few days.

3   The Rannoch Moor Lifeboat

Some of our rescues seem outstandingly funny at the time, yet, as the years pass, one forgets many of the spontaneous jokes and amusing circumstances. But recaptured memories can be rewarding, especially of occasions such as the Rannoch Moor rescue of 1965.

Two professors from Edinburgh had been fishing on the lochs of the moor; since fishing is very much a solitary occupation they had separated and agreed to meet again at 5 p.m. and return together to their car which was parked on the main road. They had both planned to return to Edinburgh the same evening, after dining at the Kings House Hotel. We first suspected that something was amiss when Doris Elliot telephoned me from the hotel to say that one of the professors had come back to the hotel, having failed to make contact with his colleague.

Most of the team members had assembled at the hotel by 8 p.m. The professor gave us details of where he had last seen his companion, a point some four miles north of the A82, across a wild and boggy section of the moor. We had several rescue dogs amongst the company and decided to deploy them in searching over the vast area which lay to the west of the line that the professors had taken on their outward journey to the fishing grounds on Loch Laidon.

Walter Elliot, George Cormack, Hugh McColl and Eric Moss all took the path, intending to search the area where the professor was last seen by his companion – about a mile from their proposed rendezvous. Willie Elliot and I were going to search the ground to the west of the path, using three dogs: Willie had Corrie, a working Border collie and a trained rescue dog; I had Tiki and Rangi, my two Alsatians. We understood that John Grey and Denis Barclay, fellow team members, would join us when they arrived.

Jimmy Ross was then our local police constable and George Cormack, a tall, dark policeman, was his assistant. Sadly, Jimmy and George were not always in perfect accord with one another! On this occasion Jimmy Ross remained at base, providing a fixed point with the flashing blue light of the police Land Rover from which we could take our bearings if we became lost. A traverse of the moor is daunting, even in daylight, as numerous detours have to be made amongst the myriads of deep, boggy streams. By night, trying to make any progress there can be a heartbreaking task.

Each of our groups had a police walkie-talkie since, at the time, our team possessed none. After about an hour Jimmy informed us that both John Grey and Denis Barclay had arrived and were setting off in the direction which Willie and I had previously taken. We flashed our torches until they had located and joined us. There was now no sign of the Land Rover or the flashing light.

'I bet he's away for a cup of coffee at the hotel,' said Willie in disgust.

'Well, if he brings some back for us it won't be so bad,' I answered. 'I could do with a cup at the moment; it's ruddy cold.'

Just then Jimmy's voice came over the walkie-talkie, 'Hello there, Hamish. Come in, please.'

'Yes, Jimmy?' I replied. 'We were missing you – where's your flashing light?'

'I had to go to the hotel to telephone,' he explained. 'Can't contact head-quarters from here. I'll be back in position shortly. Is there anything to report?'

'Negative here,' I returned. 'Just an abundance of bog. Denis and John Grey have joined forces with our party.'

'Hello, George. Hello, George. Report your position, please,' requested Jimmy.

There was no reply. The message was repeated for the next three or four minutes. At last the exasperated voice of George came over the air, 'My position at the moment is four feet deep in a bog. Two minutes ago it was five feet deep in a bog. Out!'

We had a good laugh over this, picturing the six-feet-four-inches George wallowing in a bog hole.

Working north and west we continued our 'sweep' search; the three dogs quartered the ground ahead, with John on one flank and Denis on the other. Our torches stabbed over black peat hags and tortured remains of the roots of the great Caledonian pines which at one time covered this desolate tract of moorland. Some historians say that the last wolf in Britain was killed on this moor when it was still afforested. There are two theories regarding the dis-appearance of the forest. One, that it was burned down to get rid of the wolves; the other, that it was burned to rid the area of robbers. That night my large Alsatian, Rangi, looked every inch a wolf as he weaved in and out of the peat bogs, jumping streams and giving an occasional growl.

We were beginning to grow tired and were certainly all wet – in varying degrees – when George's voice came over the walkie-talkie, 'We've got him!'

'What was that?' Jimmy demanded hastily. I could visualise him suddenly starting and becoming officious. 'Repeat your message, please, George,' he requested formally.

'We have found the missing man. Will report further in a few minutes.'

That night, Hugh had our only searchlight, which, due to loose connections, had been flickering off and on – more off than on unfortunately. It had been cursed liberally because, each time the brilliant light went out, the night seemed darker than ever. During one of their illuminated periods Hugh thought he saw something, but it was lost in the enveloping darkness as the light failed yet again. When it came on again he managed to pick out what had previously attracted his attention. It looked like a dismembered head, suspended ten feet above the bog.

'Hey look, chaps. What's that?' he called in amazement. As they approached they heard a strange noise, 'E, E, E, E, E.'

'Cripes,' said Walter. 'It must be a bloody banshee!'

Drawing closer, they saw that the suspended 'head' was the missing man's woollen hat, raised aloft on the end of his fishing rod!

The professor was sitting on an old tree stump, his legs down a bog hole. He was too exhausted even to shout, but had tilted his head backwards and was using the edge of his hand to hit his throat repeatedly, while he emitted a high-pitched scream. This produced the intermittent eerie call which they had heard. Although he saw them approaching, he was too weak to get up and come towards them. Hugh said afterwards that he had hurt his ankle and was obviously suffering badly from exposure. George immediately contacted us on his walkie-talkie.

'Hello there, Hamish,' he called. 'It looks as if this chap has hurt his ankle and won't be able to walk far. We can probably help him a bit; can you have a stretcher sent across to us?'

'There's no one else to take it over, George. Our party will have to go back to the road to collect it. But wait a minute,' I added. 'I've an idea; just hold on a tick.' I turned to the others. 'Hey Willie, you know this part quite well. Isn't there a boat in that boatshed on Loch Ba?'

'Yes, I think there is,' he said, musing. 'By Jove, that would be a help, wouldn't it? We could take it right over to the far side of the loch. Just think – the inland lifeboat service!'

'I used that boat last year when I was fishing,' said Denis. 'It belongs to the Flemings at Black Mount.'

'Oh, they won't mind us using it,' I answered.

'Hello, George,' I called. 'Do you think that you could get the prof. to the north end of Loch Ba? We can arrange to meet you there.'

'Righto,' he replied. 'We'll try. Perhaps he'll feel better when he takes some glucose and gets moving.'

'Fine,' I said. 'Standing by.'

I hadn't mentioned the boat to them as I didn't want to raise false hopes, for we still had to get it out of a padlocked boathouse.

'I tell you what,' I spoke to the others, 'I'll go back to the Land Rover and try to find some suitable tools for breaking and entering. I'd see you at the boat-house – you'd better shine a light when you reach it, though; I'm not sure exactly where it is!'

'Oh, we'll find it,' replied Denis. 'There's a wee path going over to it.'

'Be seeing you,' I called as I set off with the two dogs.

When I reached the Land Rover, Jimmy was standing outside, stamping his feet on the road.

'Well, thank goodness they've found him,' he began. 'There's nothing worse than being at base on a night like this.'

'Isn't there, Jimmy?' I asked somewhat ironically. 'Have a look at me!'

I was covered in thick, black peat from the chest down.

'Aye, you certainly do look a bit mucky,' Jimmy grudgingly admitted. 'Do you want the stretcher?'

'Yes,' I replied. 'But first of all we could do with a big tyre lever, or perhaps an ice axe if you've got one?'

'What on earth are you wanting those for?' he asked suspiciously.

'To break into the boatshed,' I answered casually. 'We need the boat to take the prof. back.'

'But man, you can't do that. It's breaking and entering!'

'Aye, and it will be taking the boat as well,' I added with a grin. 'But it's the easiest way.'

In the back of the Land Rover I discovered a suitably heavy tyre lever. Then, shouldering the stretcher, I made my way to the boathouse.

'Over here,' called Willie, flashing his light.

Beyond the light I could see the black lustre of the loch and, as I approached, the faint outline of the boathouse was visible.

There was splashing in the water.

'Don't tell me you've got the boat out already?' I asked.

'Oh, yes,' replied John Grey, passing an oar down to Denis. 'Denis has had good training at this sort of thing. He had the padlock off before we even arrived here.'

'All it requires is a bit of know-how,' retorted Denis, rather hurt by the implication. 'I remembered that I had my short metal ice axe in my pack. Anyway, it soon did the trick.'

'Well, we can't all go in that tub,' I said, eyeing the rowing boat with distrust.

'I'm quite willing to stay,' said Denis. 'I could do with a doze in the boatshed for an hour or two. I've got a big job to do tomorrow at the ski-tow and some shut-eye wouldn't do me any harm.'

'All right,' I answered. 'Then the three of us will put ourselves in the hands of the Ancient Mariner here.'

They all knew that I meant John Grey. John had recently purchased a Baltic schooner and started a freight service on the west coast. His first voyage, bringing the boat across from Norway, was in itself an epic, for they did the trip in a series of force eight and nine gales. However, the initial crew were fishermen and the boat weathered the storm well. This also proved to be only a foretaste of what was to come during its short and hectic life in Scottish waters. John's subsequent adventures round this rugged and dangerous coast could fill a book which would rival the tales of Para Handy. The stately three-masted schooner, originally built for the Baltic wood trade, shared many a tense moment with John and his often skeletal, certainly usually inexperienced, crew. The boat was christened the *Eala Dhubh* (Black Swan) but, as you can imagine, in moments of stress it was called many other, less-endearing names.

On one occasion, as they were sailing down to Oban from Glencoe, they were hit by a violent storm. The shipping forecast had predicted force eight to nine winds for Mallin and Hebrides, but this didn't deter John, who had the utmost faith in his stout-timbered craft. The huge, single-cylinder engine was panting away and spray was cascading over the starboard side as they skirted the coast of Argyll; ahead of them lay the Island of Lismore. Ralph Pierce, who was driving the *Eala Dhubh* that day, was getting worried, for they didn't seem to be making much headway. Suddenly the engine stopped.

It was no disaster, however. They had simply run out of fuel. As if this was not an unknown hazard, John had the lads drop the anchor. Taking the small pram dinghy off the top of the wheelhouse, he dropped it over the side. The only items lacking were the oars and a can – once he had these safely aboard with him, he rowed through the high seas to the shore, while the *Eala Dhubh* bucked at her anchorage. Some locals witnessed this drama from the shore. One of them shouted as he saw the dinghy coming through the spray, 'They're abandoning ship!'

John, however, had no intention of abandoning anything. He rowed ashore to the jetty at Port Appin and, after purchasing a can of diesel fuel, rowed straight back to the boat to continue the voyage.

John is a great lover of folk music and a fine singer and the villages of the west coast always open their doors to those who enjoy a good ceilidh. There was one small fishing village which was renowned both for its conviviality and for its pride in its newly constructed jetty. John tied up at this new pier, at low tide, while he and his crew – armed with guitar and squeezebox – repaired to the nearest public house. There they entertained the locals with music and ballads until the small hours of the morning, when high tide was approaching. The appearance of an irate piermaster broke up the happy occasion. Entering the bar, which, in theory, should have closed at 10 p.m., he announced with evident agitation, 'That bloody boat with the big masts is lifting up the new jetty!'

This statement was no exaggeration: the edge of the boat had caught under the pier and, as the tide came in, was relentlessly raising the entire construction.

Robin Turner, another member of our rescue team, recalls with some trepidation a voyage he made with John to Tiree. They had a cargo of pipes aboard and, again, the voyage coincided with a violent storm. Robin, who is a keen participant of various aqua sports, compares the *Eala Dhubh's* entrance into harbour that day with a fast run on a surfboard towards a rocky shoreline. The locals at the jetty watched with amazement as the tall-masted ship suddenly appeared through the mist of spray and hurtled towards them at breakneck speed. That trip must have strained the *Eala Dhubh*, since, on a later voyage, carrying timber for the Lochaber pulp mill, she started to leak badly and it was probably only her cargo which kept her afloat as she limped into Loch Linnhe.

Eventually the *Eala Dhubh* met her untimely end on the Isle of Mull, when John, who was filling a small running generator with petrol, accidentally spilt some and it caught alight. Within minutes the wooden boat was blazing furiously. Luckily no one was injured, but it was the end of the *Eala Dhubh's* glorious career. John doesn't seem to have much imagination when it comes to his personal exploits, for he tends to dismiss the most hair-raising adventures in an off-hand sentence or two. He has now acquired a new fishing boat to replace the hapless *Eala Dhubh*. John is a great asset to our rescue team, for he's always fit and strong and, though he hasn't done much climbing, he never has difficulty in following up the most treacherous route in bad conditions.

'Well, I suppose I'll have to row,' he said, picking up the oars and pulling on them with the easy rhythm that marks an experienced boatman. As we left the shore a figure with a torch joined Denis at the boatshed. It was Colin Cameron, a policeman who had just arrived from Oban. We experienced some difficulty, navigating the waters of Loch Ba in the middle of the night, but in about an hour we thought we must be nearing the north end of the loch.

'Hello, George,' I called over the walkie-talkie. 'Can you read me?'

'Yes, Hamish, I can, and I can see a strange light on the loch!'

'Aye, that's us,' I confirmed, chuckling. 'The Rannoch Moor Lifeboat crew are on their way to pick up the injured man.'

'Trust you blokes to find an easy way,' he grumbled. 'I suppose we'd have to walk back?'

'That is quite correct, Police Constable Cormack,' I returned. 'Members of the public, or the police force, will not be permitted on board!'

Our laughter echoed across the still water of the loch.

It was almost light before we neared the boathouse again. We had been rowing on a direct course towards the light which Denis had hung up at the boathouse; John was now navigating from the bows. There came a grating noise under the boat.

'Hey, John, you've grounded us,' shouted Willie who was in the stern.

'It's just that there isn't enough water below the boat; there's a wee island here,' explained John. 'Take her astern, Hamish, and we'll try farther to the east, round the other side.'

It was my stint at the oars so I eased the boat out into deeper water and we rounded the island, presently drawing alongside the boathouse.

A figure on the bank shouted, 'Have you anything to declare?'

It was Colin Cameron, a born comedian, calling to us in his best official manner.

'One injured professor,' returned Willie cheerfully.

'Well,' replied Colin, 'the duty will be a few drams at the hotel. Payment may be deferred until such time as it may be required!'

By the time we had secured the professor on the stretcher, the others had walked back from the north side of the loch to join us. Jimmy had managed to take the Land Rover almost all the way down to the boathouse, so it was only a short carry by stretcher. By some act of providence, Eric Moss had remained quite dry until then; when he saw the Land Rover's lights ahead he sighed with relief, for he shares the Highlander's aversion to getting wet. But the lights must have distracted him momentarily and he suddenly plunged chest-deep into a slimy bog; as usual, this provided a merry diversion for the rest of the team.

It is likely that the professor would have been in an extremely serious condition by morning, had he not been found, yet when we arrived safely back at Kings House he was already much recovered and we knew that he would suffer no serious after-effects from his adventure. However, he retired to bed almost immediately, after arranging that Mr MacDonald, the manager of the hotel, should provide us with sandwiches, tea and whisky. Angus MacDonald would have done so in any case, as he always helped our team in every possible way.

Most of us were standing in our underpants and socks in front of a big wood fire in the main lounge, since our outer clothing was in such a state. Denis, however, had returned to the Land Rover for his pipe and came back into the room, still wearing his clothes and boots. Suddenly realising his error, he quickly removed his boots – a deluge of peaty water spread over the rich carpet.

'Ah well,' he said with a cheerful grin. 'We all make mistakes some time or other!'

'Not bad whisky, this Talisker,' said Walter, licking his lips appreciatively. 'You were just telling me something about this whisky when we found the prof., George. What was the story?'

'Oh, yes,' replied George, laughing. 'I was about to illustrate what a fine bunch of law-enforcement officers and detectives you have in these parts!'

Willie let out a loud guffaw. 'Tell us another, George – the "sheer luck" squad?'

'Anyhow,' continued George, ignoring the interruption and settling himself in a large easy-chair. 'A case of whisky was stolen from one of the local pubs – not this establishment, I may add – and we had a fair idea who had taken it: a local fisherman. I'll not mention the name of this alcoholic character, but he's five feet two inches and has a red beard. We had no evidence, you understand, but we knew him to be a man of limited intellect and I had just a hunch that he was responsible. So I tried on him a technique which I have developed for such thefts. I call it the "Brand Denial Test". I asked him, quite forcibly' – here I could just imagine the six-feet-four-inches George towering over the unfortunate man – 'with the correct amount of intimidation in my voice: "Did you steal that case of Talisker from the pub?" "No, no, it wasn't me," the red-bearded man cringed. "It was Dewar's whisky that I took – I never touched any Talisker!"'

Our laughter was long and loud and some, at least, of the slumbering guests must have been awakened in time to see a cloudless dawn.

4 Dalness Gully Rescue

One of the difficulties of running a charitable organisation is that money has to be collected for its operation. In this respect an active rescue team, as well as having to conduct a considerable number of evacuations which can be hard on equipment and ropes, must also raise the money for these necessary items and their frequent replacement.

After a winter of regular rescue work, which was frustrated to a large extent by our lack of suitable radio communications, we realised that we would have to think of some way of raising sufficient money for the purchase of a number of walkie-talkies to provide an adequate means of communication between all our team members.

We had several good walkie-talkies available from the police and I had special permission to keep one permanently in my house, ready for immediate use. These operated on two police frequencies but were not tuned to the civilian frequency for mountain rescue. This frequency was the one in regular use by all mountain-rescue services, including the RAF, and some of the RAF rescue helicopters also could now tune into it.

We needed about six good walkie-talkies urgently.

Robin Turner, a fair-haired, bespectacled man of medium height, had come to live in the glen a few years previously and we soon discovered that he had a fund of diverse and imaginative ideas. Not only was Robin a mathematician and photographer, but he had many other accomplishments and was keen on most outdoor sports, including climbing.

A mountaineer moving into Glencoe cannot simply join our team. He has to be invited. This is not because of any superior or snobbish attitude on our part, but it ensures that we only have members who will work in complete harmony with the rest of us. We don't have an official meeting and decide the issue in cold blood; usually such a 'nominee' finds himself out on a call-out on some occasion – as any climber, even one visiting the glen, is liable to be – and his ability and attitude to the work is duly noted by the lads.

Robin had been out on a number of rescues with us and was by this time a fully fledged member of the team. He was asked if he had any ideas on how to raise some money quickly – other than diverting the team's talents from rescue to robbery. He had one suggestion right away – an airbed race. In fact he had brought this up some time previously but then, when the funds were not so low, I wasn't very keen on it. Now we were all eager to consider any reasonable means by which the walkie-talkies could be bought.

Robin outlined his scheme and stated, furthermore, that he was willing to devote all his time to organising the considerable amount of planning and artistic work in connection with it. At that time Robin was endeavouring to get plans passed for a bunkhouse in which he hoped to run folk evenings and form a base for climbers in the Glen – a much-needed building. Unfortunately this was later turned down by the planning authorities.

Several of our team members, including Jim McArtney, Phil Johnson and John Grieve, had been perfecting the art of 'airbedding' (that is, propelling themselves down the rapids on inflatable beds) for some time. It was proving a very popular pastime in wet weather, when the River Coe turned into a raging torrent. I'm afraid it wasn't my cup of tea and I kept well clear in case I was inveigled into participation.

The great event was planned to take place during the September weekend, 1969. The men's course would cover the stretch of water between my house at the Meeting of the Three Waters and Clachaig Hotel, crossing Loch Achtriochtan en route. The ladies' course was to be shorter. It would start from the eastern shore of Loch Achtriochtan; crossing this and negotiating the lower section of white water, it was some one and a half miles less than the men's course.

Besides the main event – the airbed race – other fringe entertainments had to be planned, such as the evening discotheque and the ceilidh. We even built a 'monster' for the occasion, but the placing of this in Loch Leven was left too late and we were still trying to get it floating correctly near the Burial Isles when we were caught by darkness.

The 'beast' was some forty feet long with humps which were made from large inner tubes, each weighed down at one point; the whole length of it was held together by a steel tubing keel about six inches under water. The head was a work of primitive art in red paint and Hiduminium alloy.

Not only were we too late in placing this for a sensational press viewing the following morning, but we ran out of petrol for the outboard on the way back and had to row the army dinghy, which we had borrowed, back to the shore. All was not lost, however, for the monster was rescued the following day from close to the island, the burial place of the MacDonalds of Glencoe, and transported to Loch Achtriochtan, where it looked most contented, anchored to a large submerged boulder.

The national press are always very helpful in giving our money-making stunts publicity and we were receiving donations even before the great airbed race took place. One of these, from two elderly ladies who wished to remain anonymous, was enough to pay for five walkie-talkies; I took delivery of them on the day of the airbed race. The police had brought them over for us from

Bridge of Orchy where they had arrived by passenger train.

The first job for which they were used was marshalling the airbed race, but little did we know that within two days they were to play a vital part in one of the most difficult rescues ever carried out in Scotland.

The September weekend is usually one of our busiest times in the Glen. That weekend was no exception, and the weather was superb. There had been no rain for weeks and the river was unbelievably low; so low, in fact, that to hold the race seemed a bit of a farce. I didn't think this, however, for I realised that, had we held the event in high water conditions, several people might have been injured and event organisers are never popular if they cancel their programme at the last minute.

We had pipe bands, and schoolchildren from far and wide selling our programmes. The Red Cross provided first-aid facilities and all the girls who frequent the glen, with many of the team members' wives, helped in the tea tent. Even Huan Findlay's donkey was put to task in providing rides for the children.

Much of the fun of running an event of this kind lies in the preparation; many hours of amusement and laughter went into thinking out songs and making special airbeds. Some even had tandem beds, where the first chap on the bed provided arm power and the chap behind, leg power. Ian Clough went down on a rubber duck, while Huan Findlay elected to travel on truck inner tubes, complete with his shepherd's crook. During some of their more frivolous moments, the work-team in Robin's cottage composed, amongst other 'artistic' endeavours, the following verses:

The Coe River Race

On the 30th of August in the year of '69,
The Airbed Race contestants shivered on the starting line;
This pneumatic race aquatic hardly made them look ecstatic,
But they went swirling down the river when the starter gave the sign.

Now Ossian the Bard, from his cave on Aonach Dubh,
Rode the rapids on a stag, quite a daring thing to do;
But alas it would appear, he had chosen a bum steer,
And he sank with one last 'Och' beneath the Loch.

Rabbie Burns pumped up a haggis, I'm sure you've read his ode,
On the Chieftain of the Pudden Race he perilously rode;
But alas this weathered bladder burst inside the salmon ladder,
And the pieces flew as far as Glasgow Road.

The Campbells thought they'd enter in a yellow submarine,
At first they thought it easy though propelling it upstream;
At the Clachaig main-road juncture they sadly had a puncture,
It was Rory[1] in a fury with a supersonic beam.

The occasion proved to be a great success: it fulfilled its purpose in giving people an enjoyable day in the superb setting of Glencoe and in enabling us to purchase the urgently needed radios. These would, no doubt, in the course of the next few years help to expedite the evacuation of some of the actual participants of the race, for many were climbers.

On 1 September 1969, a superb summer's day, I was catching up with work after the disruption of the airbed race. I was in my workshop completing some stretcher orders for overseas. John Grey had just called on his return from Glasgow; we were about to have a cup of tea when the telephone rang.

'Hello, is that you, Hamish?'

The voice, even with its urgent undertones, sounded familiar but before I could identify it the speaker continued, 'This is Alex Morrison. We're in a bit of bother: two of my mates have fallen in the Central branch of Dalness Gully and you'll need to get the team out.'

'Where are you speaking from, Alex?'

'I'm at the telephone box in Kings House at the moment,' he replied. 'I've just rushed up from Glen Etive.'

'Okay. Give me the rundown on what's happened.'

'Well, there were four of us in the Gully, two parties of two. I was leading with Roger Lavill while Derrick Grimmitt and Roger Clark were following behind. I was up to the Barrier Pitch, in the Central Fork, when the others came to grief. I'm not sure what happened but they both fell to the bottom of that pitch and they're still there. Both are injured, may be quite bad, head and chest injuries, I think; Roger seems to have back injuries. You'll remember Derrick?' he added. 'He used to work at Kings House.'

'Oh, yes,' I replied. 'I vaguely remember Derrick; I hope he'll be all right. See you at Alltchaorunn in about twenty minutes.'

I phoned Kathleen Findlay and Sandy Whillans and our usual call-out procedure was put into operation. For once, everyone seemed to be at home and the full rescue team was available or, rather, would be in about an hour. Meanwhile, six of us met at the roadside at the foot of the climb, which is three miles down Glen Etive on the east face of Stob na Broige, the last and most southerly peak of Buachaille Etive Mor. John Grey had driven Catherine and myself down in his car.

Dalness Gully was one of the last great gullies in the country to be climbed.

---

1 Our team member and publican whose distrust for Campbells is based on a misunderstanding in 1692.

It had repulsed many attempts in the post-war years and there had been at least one dramatic fall during an early attempt. Many of these onslaughts were made by members of the Lomond Mountaineering Club, who, by sheer persistency, had established prior rights over the great Left Fork; this is the main branch, for the gully divides into three a short way above the road. All three branches have now been climbed. The Central Fork, the one described in this rescue, was first ascended by a party led by Jim Marshall from Edinburgh in 1952 and the Right Fork was first climbed by Don Whillans and myself in 1959.

Tommy MacGuinness, a Glaswegian and member of the Lomond MC, was engaged on a serious attempt on the Left Fork one Saturday afternoon in the spring of 1950. He had run out over 100 feet of rope and his second was standing at the bottom of this great 150-foot pitch, looking anxiously up as Tommy tried to climb a particularly loose and steep section. About thirty feet below him he had put on a running belay; that is, he had put a loop of rope round a spike of rock, with a karabiner clip attached to it, through which the climbing rope ran. He was in fact 'stitched' to the mountain by his runner.

It was not entirely unexpected when a hold came away, but the subsequent effect was. He shot down with a cry, passing his runner, and with a sickening jerk the rope tightened. In those days hemp or manilla was used for climbing and if you survived such a fall without the rope breaking you counted yourself lucky. Tommy's luck held because his second, acting as a counterweight, shot upwards as Tommy went down, and they passed each other en route. Happily, neither was much the worse for the 'ups and downs' of the day! Some twenty years later Tommy came to work at the Glencoe ski tow and became an active member of our rescue team. This Left Fork was eventually climbed in 1957 after a concerted effort by John Cunningham and myself and two friends from Greenock – Sam Jagger and Charlie White.

Alex Morrison was waiting for us in Glen Etive and told us exactly where the accident had occurred. We foresaw no great difficulty, other than technical climbing, in reaching his friends, Derrick and Roger. Alex himself was well known to us because after he had left RAF Leuchars Mountain Rescue Team he had instructed with me during a period when I ran winter courses in conjunction with the SYHA, and later, while working at Clachaig Inn, he became a member of our rescue team.

There were quite a few in the advance party that day. We carried a couple of ropes, a number of pitons and some first-aid equipment. I had with me, also, one of our new walkie-talkies; Sandy had one of the police sets. At base we left PC Robin MacDougal and were in touch with him constantly.

When I had climbed the gully previously I had entered from the bottom. Now, for some reason or other, it is fashionable to enter above the junction, thereby missing out some exacting pitches. I was not sure of the 'illegal' entry point but after a couple of abortive attempts down very precipitous ground

I found the correct line in, just below the point where the Central Fork breaks off to the right from the main branch in a steep series of steps. The Right Fork branches away from the Left lower down the gully.

There were a lot of climbers in the glen that Monday. Many were rock climbers with vast experience; as the call went out to our members, they too were alerted. Over the walkie-talkie I had asked for about 2,000 feet of rope, two stretchers and quantities of pitons and slings. Soon the single-track Glen Etive road was busy with a continuous stream of cars and Land Rovers, creating problems of congestion as willing helpers hurried to the spot.

Meanwhile, we had entered the gully and reached a steep, short pitch down which a rope was hanging – Alex had told us that he had double-roped down one of the difficult pitches and had left his rope. My walkie-talkie, which was being used to pass messages to and fro, came to life again, 'Hello, Hamish; hello, Hamish. Sunshine here, come in please.'

'Hello, Sunshine. Where did they dig you up?'

'Oh, we were on exercise in the Mamores and got the call via the police. Anything you particularly want in a hurry?' Sunshine (Rae Sefton) was the leader of the Leuchars Mountain Rescue Team.

'Ropes, pegs, a stretcher and some more first aid will do for the present. We're going to need a lot of rope and if you've a couple of 500-footers these would be very handy.'

'I'll see what I can do. I think I can find you them all right.'

'Great,' I answered. 'I'll keep in touch.'

Presently we heard a shout at the edge of the gully and we could now see some more of our team. In front of them, just coming into view round a steep corner below, was John Grey.

'Hello,' Sandy shouted down. 'What's keeping you blighters? You're getting slow.'

'It's because we have to carry all the bloody equipment,' retorted John good-naturedly.

Who carries what is always a topic for discussion on a rescue and quite often members are to be seen testing the weight of their companions' rucksacks. Usually the searchlight is palmed off on some gullible volunteer, for not only does it weigh over twenty-five pounds but, from time to time, acid leaks out, ruining both the rucksack and the bearer's apparel, besides – if he is thin-skinned – burning the area best suited for sitting upon! Cunningly enough, the rucksack looks invitingly small when it is on the ground, awaiting an unsuspecting voluntary porter; the climber, lifting it, gets a shock feeling its weight but he can't very well put it down again and lose face amongst his companions. This may be the reason why we seem to go through a great number of searchlights in the course of a year, for I feel sure that vengeance is wrought upon them by disillusioned and exhausted climbers!

When Ian Clough got the call-out he had visitors – Brian Robertson, a small active climber who had done many routes in the glen and had just returned from the Yosemite Valley in California, and Phil Watkins, an able climber, editor of the magazine *Rock Sport*. They had contacted other competent climbers so that, by the time we were approaching the pitch below where the two injured men lay, we had learnt via the walkie-talkie that a vast number of rock 'tigers' had left the road and were now on their way up.

Above the steep fixed-rope pitch the gully turns almost ninety degrees to the right and enters the steep defile of the Central Fork; this was an easy section on friable rock. Ahead of us was a dead end above a chimney pitch, but on closer examination a continuation appears running up to the left, levelling out for a short distance, then springing up in a very narrow, vertical waterfall pitch, the top of which overhangs slightly. Above this again there is a short, level ledge the size of a small carpet. It was here, Alex told us, that Derrick and Roger were lying.

'Hello there,' a shout came from above.

'That's the lads there,' pointed Davy Crabb. We could see a figure on the ledge, dwarfed by a great sweep of rock down which water was pouring – the Barrier Pitch. This is one of the most exacting parts of the climb because it rises almost vertically and is composed of poor rock with no sound belays.

John Hardy and Alan Fyffe decided to go up the gully, while I suggested that I should try a new variation to the right, up vegetated rock which was very steep and probably more dangerous than the proper route. Sandy Whillans and Walter Elliot decided to come with me. I started climbing and put on the rope where the rock became steeper, leaving the end behind me on a rocky ledge for Sandy to pay out when he came up. I then climbed a difficult rocky groove which offered holds only in the form of weak tufts of grass; if one kept climbing at a reasonable speed they provided holds for a brief duration. The crack rapidly became denuded as I ascended. I reached the ledge where the climbers were, just ahead of Alan who was straddling, with obvious concern, the large chockstone which formed the lip of the pitch.

It wasn't until much later that I got all the details of that fine summer's day when the four men climbed up into Dalness Gully. Here, Roger Lavill describes what happened:

> Alex Morrison, Roger Clark, Derrick Grimmitt and myself, following the advice of the guidebook, walked up the true left bank and entered the gully about the point where the first fork occurs. We had been to the pub the night before and I suppose that we started a bit later than we intended. We climbed several short pitches and, keeping to the right at the next fork, we gained the Central branch, eventually arriving at the base of

the Great Barrier pitch. So far we had been climbing in two ropes of two, but for the harder pitches we all roped together.

At the bottom of this great pitch we stopped for a bite to eat. The sun had just reached us over the steep right wall as we looked out of the gully and it was lovely and warm. We were sitting beside a pool on the warm boulders. Little did we know as we drank this crystal clear water that Derrick would almost end his life in it a short time afterwards.

'We'll keep all these meat pies and cake for later,' said Roger as he repacked them into his rucksack.

'I certainly don't want one just now. How about you, Alex?'

'No thanks.'

I recalled reading an account of the first ascent of this gully in an old issue of *Mountaincraft*, a mountaineering magazine now out of print. I remembered that this pitch had been climbed on the left-hand side but I could see a very ancient hemp sling on the right wall on a ledge about thirty feet up. Furthermore, the back right-hand side of the pitch seemed to me to be the logical line so I decided to have a go at this. I climbed up to the old sling and the others gave loud laughs when I picked it off the rock bollard and it promptly disintegrated. I threw it down at them. Just then a large bird appeared; probably a golden eagle.

'You chaps had better watch out,' I yelled to them jokingly. 'That's a bloody vulture.'

'Why don't you get your finger out and get up that pitch?' retorted Alex, sunning himself but watching my rope.

Once I had put a nylon tape runner in place of the old one I began to traverse left into the steep groove. This, I soon discovered, was quite hard and I ended up forcing it by using two or three pitons. The last piton was a thin knife-blade peg which went in only about half an inch and wasn't very secure. To minimise the leverage on it I put a small loop of nylon tape round the blade of the piton, close to the rock, rather than put a karabiner clip through the eye which would increase the leverage. Once I had put this last peg in, though it wasn't very safe, it made the remaining section of the groove much easier for me. When I eventually reached a point where I could take the others up – a small ledge – I had great trouble in finding any form of belay to which to tie myself. However, I did manage to get two further pitons in and once I had clipped on to these I took Alex up. The tied-off peg still held when Alex used it. Before I moved off Derrick had also come up, belayed by Alex. Alex was anchored at the back of the ledge. Derrick was tied to both of the pitons but was sitting sideways near the edge. This, we all agreed later, was a mistake.

I was some thirty feet up the next pitch when I heard a shout, followed by a jangling noise. Roger had been standing in a sling which was attached to one peg while he removed the other pitons. He had taken out all but this last peg and was just about to transfer his weight to the rock when it suddenly came out. He felt relieved as the rope tightened above him – Derrick was belaying him – but then he felt himself falling again and he said afterwards that he was amazed that this had happened. He had the most vivid recollections of the walls of the gully rushing past and the floor hurtling up to meet him. Roger weighs thirteen stone and his sudden fall dragged Derrick from his belay position over the edge. The strain went on the two pegs; when this increased, as Derrick's weight came on them as well, the pegs came out and the rock, which is very friable, broke. One of the aluminium-alloy karabiners, which has a minimum breaking strain of 1,000 kilograms, broke too; no doubt it was not subjected to this strain by the two men hanging from it but by the fact that the karabiner jammed between the peg and the rock so that the strain incurred was almost at right-angles to the backbone of the karabiner.

'The lads have fallen,' shouted Alex.

'I can climb back down all right,' I replied, feeling numbed.

Alex went to the edge and looked down. Derrick was unconscious, face down in the pool. Roger had been stunned and had just regained consciousness.

'Roger,' shouted Alex frantically. 'For Christ's sake get Derrick out of the water or he'll drown.'

By this time I had descended to Alex and we both held our breath as Roger lifted Derrick clear of the water. It was an act of providence that he was able to do this for he himself had fallen some forty feet.

Alex had some mini-flares in his rucksack and he quickly set off a red one, which described a high trajectory out of the gully. We realised that we had to get down somehow, but it was too dangerous to trust another single piton; the rock was so brittle that we couldn't rely on a peg. We decided to use two: one to double-rope and the other as a belay for the safety rope. In this way we stood a greater chance of reaching our friends below, intact. Alex went down first and the piton from which he double-roped held firm. Next I started down, using the other piton; it had a karabiner attached as a pulley for my safety rope, which was being paid out by Alex as I descended.

Halfway down it jammed! I had to undo it and could only pray that the remaining piton wouldn't come out.

At the bottom of the pitch we moved Derrick to a more comfortable position and I put a field dressing on his head. Both their helmets were badly damaged. Alex set off another flare, but we decided it would be best for him to go down so I gave him a top rope for as far as possible and he abseiled down to the traverse, which the rescue party were to use to gain access to the gully later that day. We learned later that the flares had been seen by a passing tourist and reported to a local who dismissed it as 'poachers at work'.

On the ledge beside the pool, Roger's back was stiffening up – he had chipped vertebrae and was covered in bruises; Derrick came to the verge of consciousness several times. Sometimes he was deeply unconscious, then he would revive a bit and struggle and mumble. It was difficult to prevent him pulling off the dressing. Roger and I examined the battered pies in his rucksack. Undoubtedly they had gone a long way towards breaking his fall, for they were cushioning the small of his back within his rucksack; they were completely pulverised. Since that fall Roger has always carried his wife's rich fruitcake and Sainsbury's pork pies – as much for their energy-sustaining properties as for their kinetic-energy-absorbing qualities!

Derrick soon became quite vocal and, indeed, he was to keep up an intermittent stream of conversation for many days to come.

'I'm sick of this route,' was his first comment, ' ... I'm fed up, let's go down ... I'm going to be sick, I'm going to be sick.' He kept this up for so long that I got tired of it.

'Derrick, if you want to be sick, this is the place to do it.'

He only said one more word before he relapsed into a deep coma again: 'Die.'

This was the only time that I can remember being worried.

Roger must have slipped at 3.30 p.m. and I think it was about 7.30 p.m. when I heard shouts from below. Shortly afterwards I gave a top rope to a chap who was directly below, just as Hamish appeared round the true right wall on the gully.

Roger greeted us from the back of the ledge where he was belaying John Hardy. Beside him Derrick was lying flat on the boulders, his head red with blood.

'Derrick doesn't look too good,' I observed. I fixed the rope for Sandy to use as a handrail; after he was up safely, Walter tied on to the end of it and Sandy belayed him.

Meanwhile I had gone over to Derrick at the base of the rock pitch. His condition appeared serious and I was immediately alarmed. It was obviously going to be an epic task to get him down. I asked Roger if it would be possible for him to take his companion down on a top rope while we dealt with Derrick.

'Yes, I can try,' he said.

'Anyhow, there will be any number of people coming up; you'll just have to yell for assistance if you require it.'

'Righto, then I'll be off. Come on, Roger.'

Derrick was suffering mainly from head injuries; other than dress these and get him into the casualty bag which we had just pulled up on a rope, there wasn't much we could do. He was unconscious so we made sure that his airway was clear; John Hardy and Sandy kept an eye on him to make sure that he didn't vomit and that his tongue didn't fall back in his throat.

Alan, Wall Thompson and I were meanwhile looking for some sort of rock belay for the rope. There were no anchorage points in the gully and, though we had some special thin pitons, made from metal used on spacecraft, we could only get them in a short way. However, Wall did find a jammed chockstone belay through which we threaded a section of nylon rope.

There were more people gathered below now. John Grey had a radio and was in touch with base. I had another, but it was in my pack and we didn't have time to use it just then. Dudley Knowles was busy rolling cigarettes for those who smoked, since he was the only one with dry tobacco.

I shouted down to John Grieve, asking him to go up over the side of the gully at the point where it turns through ninety degrees and try and fix an anchor on a tree the other side; I knew of this tree from previous visits to the gully. John Grieve was a new member of our team and this was his first big rescue as a team member. He took an end of a 500-foot rope and climbed the very loose wall opposite us. John Hardy, still keeping an eye on Derrick, lowered his own rope down the pitch and the other end of the 500-foot rope was tied to it. When this was hauled up we were in a position to tie it to the belays we had obtained. John sent his rope down again and the end of a further 500-foot rope was tied on. This we pulled up until the halfway mark was just leaving the level bed of the gully on the lower pitch. I then asked Huan Findlay and Willie Elliot to tie on the stretcher which had been brought up by Huan and Davy Crabbe. When this was done we hauled up the stretcher.

On the ledge I rigged up two suspension slings for it and attached to these two pulleys. The middle of the second 500-foot rope was attached to the suspension slings and the stretcher was then ready to clip on to the other 500-foot rope, once John had found the belay over the wall of the gully opposite us.

A muffled shout indicated that he had managed to do this; a few moments later he appeared again on the edge of the gully wall and told us that it was fixed to a tree some sixty feet below. He had used another rope – attaching it to the tree – which ran up to where he was standing on the edge; a karabiner clip, through which the 500-foot rope now passed, was attached to a loop on this rope. He proceeded to sort out this section of rope so that it hung free to the party underneath him.

The plan was to lower Derrick on the suspension rope down and out from the pitch we were standing on, so that he would reach a point halfway along the level section of gully below, where the others were waiting.

When I asked for full tension on the suspension rope it whipped into life, for they had let it go slack while we clipped on to it the pulleys from the stretcher. We let the stretcher out over the edge at a time when Derrick's breathing was regular and even. We wouldn't have risked sending him down had there been a chance of him vomiting or requiring resuscitation. There is always an element of risk in mountain-rescue work, however, both for the patient and for the rescuers. Had we lowered him down this pitch in the conventional manner, it would have meant tilting the stretcher up, so that it hung vertically down the pitch. Such tactics, with Derrick's present condition, might well have killed him. The method we decided upon was the only way to ensure that he had a fair chance of survival, for he would remain horizontal throughout the evacuation.

As the weight of the stretcher was taken by the suspension rope, it sagged a bit and the stretcher went down over the edge, though still quite horizontal.

'Slacken on suspension rope.'

'Okay,' shouted Huan.

'Keep slackening off on it,' I continued.

'Right, Hamish,' the reply came from below.

Beside me, Walter was tied to the back of the gully and was carefully releasing the rope through a figure-of-eight device. Wall was holding Walter in place, for the peg belay to which he was attached wasn't too safe.

The party directly below, who held an end of the second 500-foot rope attached to the stretcher, were taking it in as the stretcher was lowered. It descended smoothly, like a hovercraft, and in a matter of minutes was being fielded by the remainder of the party in the bed of the gully.

'Slacken off,' someone yelled from below.

All the ropes went slack.

'He's down.'

Catherine came on over the radio, asking for regular pulse checks on Derrick and warning us that a very wary eye should be kept on him. Sandy and Robin Turner were delegated this task – both Sandy and Alan Fyffe were already down the pitch, having double-roped off just after Derrick had reached the gully bed. In a very short space of time we all joined them. John Hardy came last, throwing down both ends of the 500-foot ropes to the others below.

I shouted up to John Grieve that we would still use his belay for the next stage of the evacuation, a semi-suspended 'lower' at right angles to the previous one, down to a pitch where Ian Clough and Brian Robertson were now established. Ian had come up with Brian and Phil Watkins and some other English climbers and decided that he could be of more use in these lower reaches, arranging belays for the fixed-rope pitch. Brian himself had suffered very severe head injuries while attempting a solo ascent of Raven's Gully in April 1960, when he was sixteen. He had been found unconscious by a search party and it had taken him years to recover fully.

I was within shouting distance of Ian now. I suggested to him that someone should come down with the end of the 500-foot suspension rope, if he could find an anchor for it.

'I'll look around, Hamish,' he replied.

Derrick was now being carried to a point from where he could be launched on the next stage of his aerial evacuation.

It took Ian some time to get this arranged, but I didn't ask the reason for the delay; I knew that any delay would be fully justified. Ian wasn't a person to waste words. If he said he had a belay that was good, it was never questioned. He was probably the most meticulous person, regarding safety, I ever climbed with and had a wonderful knowledge of artificial climbing, knowing exactly when a piton was in securely. If he had doubts about a piton he would ensure that he had enough doubtful ones in to safeguard that particular situation in the event of a fall or sudden strain.

It seems ironical, looking back on the way he was killed on the south face of Annapurna a few years later, how chance and bad luck caught him unawares in the last few minutes of the expedition. He was probably the ideal team member in rescue work. He had a competence on the mountains both in winter and in summer which would be hard to equal. His mechanical knowledge regarding rescue work was first class and his attitude to those who were unfortunate in coming to grief was sympathetic and considerate. His loss to our team is something none of us likes to speak about for we all feel it personally.

Alan and John Hardy started to lower the stretcher down the new cableway while Ian began to take the strain by pulling the end of the 500-foot stretcher rope from below. Even with so much tension on the suspension rope, the stretcher touched the bed of the gully, which was formed in a series of jagged ribs; both Sandy and I had to go down after it to guide it over these. Presently it reached the smoother rock at the bottom of this easier-angled pitch and some of the party from below climbed up to assist us. We half-carried the still-suspended stretcher down to a safe point near the lower end of the 500-foot suspension-rope belay and unclipped it from the pulley. Derrick seemed to be all right, but was unconscious and also restless. However, he was well secured, in both the casualty bag and the stretcher. Catherine inquired about his condition and I gave her his pulse beats, which were most erratic; she suggested that I should give him another injection of cortisone. Catherine had been experimenting with the use of cortisone for badly shocked patients and the recent results had been quite dramatic. The use of this drug had been advocated by Dr Otto Trott in the western USA a number of years previously, but it hadn't been used before for mountain-rescue work in this country. I gave Derrick the injection and manoeuvred the stretcher into a launching position for the next lower down the fixed-rope pitch.

Eric Moss was below, a stalwart rescue-team member. Eric – who isn't a climber and who took to rescue 'with a vengeance' rather late in life – had trouble in climbing the fixed rope of the pitch below and gave up after several abortive attempts. He was now below with some other climbers and members of the RAF Leuchars Mountain Rescue Team. As a regular soldier, Eric served overseas for a large part of his career and reached the rank of major. He was a Japanese prisoner of war and, coincidentally, was in the same regiment as our honorary president, Brigadier Ian Stewart of Achnacon.

'Eric, watch out for the stretcher coming down,' I called. 'Ian'll take over this part of the lower.'

I was going to climb down and see how we should take Derrick out of the gully, for there were obvious problems in carrying a seriously injured man across the bad traverse line from the gully bed to its edge.

'Okay, I'll do that,' shouted Eric.

I double-roped down to where he was, while Ian was getting the ropes secured to the piton belays which he and Brian had organised.

Regular reports on Derrick were going out over the walkie-talkie to Catherine, who was on the gully bank. She asked if the RAF had any oxygen available, as our team supply was of very short duration. Sunshine, who had an RAF walkie-talkie with him, came on the air.

'I have a two-hour oxygen supply with the RAF ambulance at Kinlochleven, Catherine. I'll ask the driver at base to phone round for this.'

'That's great,' she replied.

On inspecting the exit from the gully I realised that we would have to use yet another cableway – leading from the gully bed upwards, at an angle of about ten degrees to the horizontal, to the gully bank several hundred feet away. It was obviously going to be very difficult as various trees obstructed the line and there was a corner to go round. Brian Robertson had joined me and I asked him to try and get pitons into the gully wall for the bottom attachment of the cableway. A 500-foot rope was then taken up the traverse line to the main support party on the edge; I asked them to secure this as well as possible – they would need to tension it later.

Behind me, accompanied by the crashing of rocks, the stretcher came to rest on the floor of the gully and the others started to descend. It was about half an hour before everyone was down. The long shadows of evening were stealing across the face of A'Cioch opposite: a small peak which a year previously had provided us with an all-night drama, searching for the body of a young German.

I sent one of the climbers out to the edge of the gully with the end of the 500-foot rope which was attached to the stretcher, telling him to ask the RAF and police parties to take it in when instructed. Ian attached the bottom end of the new 500-foot suspension rope to the pitons which Brian had put in and then I asked the gully-edge party to tension it to see how it would hang. It was all right for a short way while it was clear of the gully wall, but about halfway along, at a protruding rib of rock, it fouled and hung close to a rowan tree which would cause us some trouble.

We arranged that two people would go in front of the stretcher, when it came close to the rock wall, while another two took up the rear. Denis Barclay and I would hold it out when we reached the rib. Dudley Knowles and Rory MacDonald followed at the rear of the stretcher, while at the front were Huan Findlay and Eric Moss. John Grey was in 'the long field' to help it past the tree. All went well at the beginning; the stretcher hung suspended and free from the rock. Then the suspension rope sagged too much and the haulage on the stretcher rope was too slow. I shouted to Sandy, who, with Ian's group, was holding the lower stretcher rope, and asked if he would go up and sort out the shambles on the bank.

Sandy is well suited for tasks like this: having been an instructor with the marine commandos, he has the necessary sergeant-major touch for getting things done in a hurry. Indeed, his control of an avalanche-probing line is something which must be seen to be believed: discipline is imperative in such a task and usually almost impossible to enforce. In about ten minutes Sandy came on the radio and said he was ready to start again. He had managed to get a further belay higher up and had reorganised the haulage system.

'Right,' I shouted to John Grey, who had the radio and who was perched, like a hoody crow, on a thin branch of the rowan tree above a frightening drop. 'Tell him to haul away.'

With a jerk the stretcher moved upwards; we had to exert all our strength to keep it clear of the rock. When we came to the rock rib, the rope ran tightly round it and we saw that it would be very difficult to get the pulleys of the stretcher round this corner.

I left the stretcher and put a piton high above; part of the weight of the stretcher was taken on this by another rope, using the karabiner on the piton as a pulley. I asked Denis to tie himself on to the outer edge of the stretcher and then lean back, almost horizontally, to haul the stretcher free of the face as it rounded the corner. Denis is only five-feet-six inches tall and his feet failed to make contact with the rock face when he leant right back, for the rock was also undercut. Being taller, I changed places with him and managed to lift the stretcher out free from the face, with most of the stretcher's weight supported on the rope running through a karabiner at the piton above – held by Eric and Huan. It was then taken round this awkward corner.

John Grey then helped it past the rowan tree. We crossed a steep slab, which the first two climbers effectively cleared of grass tufts, which were the only footholds, so that the others had great difficulty in following. None of us had a safety rope during these manoeuvres and we were lucky that no one plunged into the depths of the lower gully, several hundred feet below.

Catherine examined Derrick and said he was worse than she had feared. She insisted that we keep him as level as possible for the next 1,000 feet down the bank of the gully. This section was by no means easy: a steep hillside with small cliffs. Besides, it was now growing dark and a few of the rescuers had already switched on their headlamps. The searchlights were unpacked and ready. We decided to lower Derrick on the 500-foot ropes as this would be much quicker than using the shorter 200-foot ones. When we were all assembled I asked that everyone not actually employed in lowering the stretcher should keep level with or below it, to prevent injury to the patient or anyone else from falling rocks. This is a continual hazard on the easier slopes, where people tend to relax and meander down after the rigours of a difficult section. The main party set off, carrying Derrick on the stretcher, keeping the front end as high as possible so that he remained level. All went smoothly for 300 feet or so, when Catherine was alarmed by a sudden deterioration in his condition. The oxygen had arrived and was administered. In a few minutes he seemed to improve and the descent continued. Eventually we all reached Dud and Robin, who had gone ahead and were lodged at a small rock face with a belay thoroughly prepared. By walkie-talkie, John Grey asked the belay party above to hold it while the change of belays was made.

Just below us, Willie was picking out the best route down with the powerful beam of the searchlight.

'You should keep to the edge of the gully,' he shouted. 'Bear right when you get down to the tree, about 500 feet down. That should make a good changing point for the next lower.'

'Okay,' shouted Wall, who was at the rear of the stretcher.

Eric Moss, who was at the front, called, 'Let's go.'

About 400 feet below, as I was crossing over towards the new stretcher belay with Sandy, there was a yell from above. It was Dud, taking up the warning cries of the top party, 400 feet above him. A great rock was coming down. We had no idea how large it was but it must have been the size of a large packing case. It bit deeply into the hillside with loud crunching noises, emitting sparks and starting associated stone falls as it hurtled between Dud and Robin, so close that Robin felt the blast of air. It shaved past Sandy and I felt that one of us must surely be hit.

Dudley recalls the incident, 'I looked down, hardly believing our lucky escape and yelling warnings to those below. They didn't need any, however, for the noise of this rock was enough to create fear in any climber's heart. We could see the lights scatter like sparks – as if a smith had hammered a piece of white-hot steel on his anvil.'

'That was close,' breathed Sandy. 'I nearly wet my pants!'

'Ruddy fools,' I muttered – but it is very easy to dislodge a rock in the dark and those above didn't all have headlamps.

We learned that Roger Clark had been carried down on a stretcher after reaching the edge of the gully and was now at the bottom, awaiting Derrick in the ambulance. Little did we know, when we asked him to double-rope down the gully, that he had two chipped vertebrae. It often happens that when one of the party has a major injury, one tends to overlook the other survivors who, in the face of their companion's extremely serious condition, tend to make light of their own injuries, which may be quite extensive.

We caught up with the stretcher, which had stopped again, to learn that Derrick's heart had stopped beating; Catherine was giving him cardiac massage and more oxygen. Presently he revived and Sandy, who was standing too close to Derrick's feet, which had some freedom of movement within the casualty bag, was suddenly kicked in his stomach, much to the amusement of the gathered throng. The evacuation took on a lighter note farther down where we could abandon belays and walk him down, using the 500-foot rope only as a back anchor. Derrick appeared to be slightly better and started shouting, 'Get a move on; get a move on, you bastards. What's keeping you?' Even when unconscious Derrick had a sense of humour!

Derrick suffered from very severe head injuries. One of the reports we received stated that his skull was a mass of fractures 'like a cracked eggshell'. He was taken to Belford Hospital, Fort William, and was seen by Mr Campbell, FRCS. Due to his critical condition he was transferred to Killearn Hospital, near Glasgow, where he was examined by Professor Bryan Jennett, department of neurosurgery. Professor Jennett stated, 'He sustained a compound depressed fracture of the skull and our teaching on this is that no immediate surgery is required and there is always time for the patient to be transferred to a central unit, as occurred in this instance. All that is required by way of temporary treatment is to clean up the area if possible and then have it adequately covered. It would seem reasonable to give immediate large doses of penicillin. He was operated on immediately on arrival and the dura was torn and the brain lacerated. However, the pieces of bone were replaced so that there would be no skull defect requiring a subsequent operation, and he made a good recovery.'

In hospital Derrick kept up his unconscious repartee. He was swearing so volubly at the nurses that a sister came up to him and told him to stop swearing, as it might upset the nurses. Derrick replied, 'How the hell can I stop swearing when these bastards bother me all the time?'

Over eighteen months later we were on a mountain-rescue exercise, showing several chief constables and Mr T. Gillette of the Home and Health Department the method of cableway evacuation which we had perfected. Just then a man whom I thought I recognised walked into our base tent. Only a few moments before Mr Kenneth MacKinnon, our chief constable, had been telling this party about the Dalness rescue, almost two years previously, during which a multiple cableway system was used.

'I'm Derrick Grimmitt,' announced the climber. 'Remember? – Dalness Gully?'

'Well, isn't that a coincidence,' I said. 'We were just talking about you!'

5   A Long Day

New Year is always a busy time in Glencoe; climbers from south of the border flock northwards to spend Hogmanay in the glen. Ambitious plans made at this festive period, with its associated lack of sleep and excesses of food and alcohol, can have serious results. Climbers tend to have definite aims and it is frequently their refusal to adapt or modify these which leads them into trouble.

It was at this season – New Year 1970–1971 – that Sandy Whillans called in to see me and remarked speculatively, 'Well, Hamish, I wonder how many we'll take down over the next few days?'

'We should run a lottery on it,' I suggested. 'Proceeds to go to the team.'

'Aye, that's a good idea,' answered Sandy, taking a long pull on his pipe while his 'police' mind worked overtime. 'But what if the chap killed won it? It could be awkward!'

His loud laugh caused my two dogs, outside, to bark. Sandy, it will be observed, has a very macabre sense of humour.

'Remember last New Year's Day, Sandy?' I recalled. 'When the two climbers were overdue from Crowberry Gully on the Buachaille?'

'I can that,' he replied, stabbing the stem of his pipe in my direction. 'And I wish we could have a few more rescues like that one. What a laugh … '

On that particular occasion, about 7 p.m. on New Year's Day, Sandy, Walter and Willie Elliot and I went up to the foot of the Buachaille to see if we could find any trace of the two climbers. They were friends of mine and I had naturally been a bit concerned when they failed to turn up that evening. We had night-glasses with us and large rockets for attracting attention, which have a vertical range of about 1,000 feet. Unfortunately, the smooth right wall of Crowberry Gully (a hard 1,000-foot ice climb of fine quality) is overhanging, so, from the main road, it can be extremely difficult to see any torch signal given from above by a distress party.

We sent up a rocket from the most advantageous position near the main road; it exploded, leaving behind it a vertical ribbon of light like a tracer bullet, and illuminated the whole face for a few seconds. We saw nothing – nor did we expect to, since the rocket was fired purely to attract the attention of the two men who were high above.

As soon as the echo had died away, I spoke through a loudhailer which we use for such emergencies and requested, 'Flash your torches if you're all right.'

In a minute or so an answering twinkle of light came from high up on the sinister iced flank of the Buachaille, more than 2,000 feet above us.

'If you're all right and do not need assistance, can you flash your light again?'

Once again, an answering twinkle.

'If you'd like some whisky, will you flash your light?' I shouted finally.

The subsequent flashes last a full two minutes!

The next day they finished the gully and returned, exposed but otherwise unscathed. We met them as they were coming down the mountain and gave them some glucose drink. They couldn't eat anything immediately for their throats were swollen due to dehydration.

Still chuckling, Sandy had just left the workshop when, at 3 p.m., the telephone rang. It was Dudley Knowles, who, with his wife Ann, had taken over the management of the Clachaig Inn. Rory MacDonald, the proprietor, had recently launched a devastating new whisky called 'Glencoe' and was occupied at the time with the promotion of its sales.

'There's a chap just come in, Hamish,' Dudley began, 'who says that his girlfriend has fallen on Stob Coire nam Beith. He thinks she has a broken leg and says that there is a party of other climbers up there with her.'

Dudley didn't believe in wasting words!

'Does she have any other injuries?' I asked.

'He says,' Dud informed me after consulting with the lad, 'that she may also have injured her back.'

I told him to ask Ann to put the call-out procedure into operation (several of the womenfolk in the glen do this, thus saving valuable time) and arrange for everyone to meet at Achnambeithach – the Elliots' house – in fifteen minutes.

'I'll contact both the police and the Elliots,' I added. However, when I contacted the Elliots I learned that the two brothers, Willie and Walter, were both in Fort William. I had trouble also in getting through to Sandy Whillans at the Glencoe police station and had to dial 999 and ask the exchange to interrupt a call which was then being made from the police station.

My rucksack was already packed with all the necessary equipment and first aid; it was only a matter of putting my boots and snow gaiters on, then driving the few miles down the road to Achnambeithach. Though it was cold, it was a good day; but I could see that the tops had that blurred, white look which indicates near-blizzard conditions on the summit.

When I arrived I went straight into our rescue truck which was parked at the Elliots' house and sorted out what would probably be required for this straightforward evacuation. By the time I had finished, a few more of the team had arrived. Dud and Sandy Whillans agreed to take turns with the stretcher while Alan Fyffe and myself went on ahead with the casualty bag and first-aid equipment, for in these wintry conditions exposure is a grave risk, especially to the injured or anyone suffering from shock.

About 4 p.m. Alan and I reached the party of six climbers; the girl was covered in down jackets and anoraks. She was lying on a ledge which had been cut out of the ice; two of these climbers were holding her in position, with their ice axes driven into the slope on the underside of her. Diagnosis of injuries in such conditions can be very difficult and this occasion was no exception; the wind had increased to full gale force and the biting blast cut at our faces like a knife. Spumes of snow, whipped up by the wind, cascaded from the ridge above high into the air, it was like being in a sandblasting cabinet. Though the injured girl, Carolyn Knight, could move her legs, she complained of bad pains in her ribs and back. I gave her some DF118 painkilling tablets when we put her into the casualty bag. By this time, Sandy Whillans had arrived with the stretcher, dressed only in his pullover and climbing breeches as, lower down, he had given Dud Knowles all his personal gear to carry.

'Cripes, I'm bleeding cold,' said Sandy. 'It would freeze a brass monkey ... How is she?' he added.

'Doesn't look too good,' I replied. She was out of earshot and the wind whipped the words away in the opposite direction from where she lay. 'But it's difficult to tell. I haven't had a good look at her yet.'

'She looks all right to me,' answered Sandy with a laugh. I handed him my anorak since I also had a duvet jacket. He was chilling very quickly after the 2,000-foot carry with the stretcher and had also hurt his back when he stumbled on his way up the icy section of the path.

We rapidly organised belays on the rock face above and, after strapping Carolyn to the stretcher, we lowered her down the remainder of the slope on long ropes. It was about 400 feet down, for she had not fallen to the bottom but had lodged on some frozen scree which was responsible for her injuries.

Walter Elliot, who had returned from Fort William with his brother Willie and had been in touch with me over the radio, mentioned that shouts of 'Help' had been reported from Buachaille Etive Mor. He thought that these reports were reliable for they had been given by a responsible climber. Accordingly I asked him, 'Can you go up with Taff Jones who is at base, and investigate this further? We'll be in touch when we come down.'

'Aye, we'll do that,' he answered. 'Taff is beside me now.'

'Fine then, we'll see you later.'

We brought Carolyn off the hill with little incident and she was sent to the Fort William hospital. We later learnt that she had lost a great deal of blood and was given a transfusion, but she recovered eventually. Some six weeks after the incident, I received a letter from her boyfriend who was with her when she fell. In his letter he assured me that they were responsible climbers, which, no doubt, they were. He also very generously suggested that he would deduct so much each week from his wages for a considerable length of time in appreciation of the Glencoe Mountain Rescue Team. Of course we had to refuse this offer, which might perhaps have caused him hardship. He did, however, send us a cheque for which we thanked him. It bounced! We never had the heart to let him know.

Before we disbanded at the Elliots' cottage, I asked the lads to keep in touch after they had had a meal: Walter had returned from Buachaille Etive Mor and he thought that he too had heard shouts for help, although he couldn't be sure, We didn't like the situation. One develops a nose for trouble in the mountains. It is a number of small points which have little significance individually that, considered together, spell danger to the experienced rescuer. I had arranged to meet Sandy, Walter and Willie at my place at 8 p.m. and we were to go up the road to Buachaille Etive Mor to see if we could gather any more information about the missing party.

We all fed well. Sandy was the first to join me, but presently we heard the deep note of our rescue truck outside, indicating the arrival of Willie and Walter. We drove up to Jacksonville car park, where I suggested that we should try the technique of the loudhailer and rocket. As I mentioned, we had been successful with this method on a rescue the previous New Year, but this night, unfortunately, a strong wind was blowing which we thought would make calling with the loudhailer ineffective. Anyhow, we sent up a maroon rocket which rose to over 1,000 feet, emitting a brilliant flash and a loud report. Once the deep reverberations had died away, I tried calling the missing climbers with the loudhailer. There was no response. I tried several times more and on one occasion Walter, whose faculties are exceptionally acute, thought he heard a call, but we could not be certain of it.

By this time Eric Moss had driven up in his Volkswagen and Taff Jones from the Ogwen Cottage team had also returned in his Land Rover. Taff, in common with quite a few other regular visitors to Glencoe, somehow always manages to become involved in helping with rescues during popular weekends. As he drew to a halt in his Land Rover I asked, 'Can you stay at base for a while, Taff, in case there are any further calls for help?'

The rest of us went off to look for the remainder of the party which was from the University of Bangor.

We met them in Glen Etive, where they had gone to ensure that the missing two (a chap and a girl) had not come off the summit of the mountain on the east side, i.e. towards Glen Etive, rather than following the more usual route down an easy corrie to Altnafeadh. We asked them when the missing pair were last seen.

'It was about 2 p.m. today, at the bottom of Crowberry Ridge,' one replied. Crowberry Ridge is a hard route in winter when covered with snow and is about 1,000 feet long. 'We saw them at the first chimney pitch and they were also seen by some others in our group who were going up Curved Ridge.' (This easier route runs parallel to and east of Crowberry Ridge.) 'We haven't seen them since.'

'How are they equipped?' I asked.

'Quite well,' answered the spokesman of the group, who appeared tall and dark in the lights of the police Land Rover. 'But they're not experienced,' he continued. 'They've one torch between them – as far as we can find out.'

We discussed the matter between ourselves and thought it prudent to wait for an hour or so, in case they were descending without a light – the torch might easily be broken.

'Could you patrol the Glen Etive road until we get back?' I asked the Bangor party. 'And if another group would return to the Lagangarbh Hut they could observe the corrie behind it, since that's the other easy way down off the top of the Buachaille.'

Then we bid them au revoir and retired to Kings House Hotel for an hour. Meanwhile, Taff Jones was keeping watch at the car park.

Kings House Hotel is owned by Robin Fleming – a relative of the late Ian Fleming of 'James Bond' fame – and he is an ardent supporter of the Search and Rescue Dog Association, as well as having a keen interest in mountain-rescue affairs. While we were having a quiet drink in the bar, a film director – Austin Campbell – came over and had a few words with us. He was shortly to make a film of the Massacre of Glencoe. Eric Moss, a keen amateur historian, immediately and somewhat petulantly questioned the authority of a Campbell to undertake this task, for Campbells are not thought much of locally. As a matter of fact, Rory MacDonald has gone so far as to have a notice printed for his hotel, stating 'No Hawkers or Campbells'. However, Eric Moss chose the wrong person for such a contention, based on local clan history; Austin proved that he had done his Massacre homework thoroughly and effectively parried all Eric's objections.

Meanwhile some of the team members had arrived: John Grey, John Grieve, Alan Fyffe, Dud Knowles and his twin brother Dave, who had had an accident himself the previous year on the Grand Dru in Chamonix, France, where he broke his leg and had to be evacuated by helicopter. This was to be his first time on the hill since that fateful event. Some of Sandy Whillans's police team had also arrived from Oban and other outlying districts; the lounge bar now took on an air of impending action. Besides our team, clad in full winter climb-ing gear, there were also two members of parliament drinking at the bar!

At about ten o'clock we all returned to the car park. Taff reported as we joined him, 'I haven't seen anything, Hamish. No lights, no cries ... nothing.'

'Well, it looks as if we'll have to go up,' I answered. 'But first we'll check the Lagangarbh Hut.'

However, we found that no word had been received there of the missing party, nor had the gamekeeper at the Altnafeadh homestead, Alasdair MacDonald, who is a member of the police team, seen or heard anything, though his young wife Rosalyn thought she had heard whistles from the Buachaille earlier in the day.

We returned once more to the Jacksonville car park. After trying again to make contact with the loudhailer and searchlight, to no avail, we decided that we would go up and investigate the area of Crowberry Ridge and Crowberry Gully. Not, I may add, a welcome thought to us on a bleak and very cold winter's night. In the Kings House we had discussed various plans in the event of the missing party not turning up. I had suggested that only three or four of us should go up to make a cursory search, as we would need to tackle technically advanced ice climbing in the dark – at least, with only the light from our headlamps and the searchlight – so I asked my climbing instructors, Alan Fyffe and John Grieve, and Dave Knowles to accompany me. However, since there was a lot of essential equipment to be taken up, I soon decided that it would be better for some of the experienced members of the Bangor group, with some more of our own team chaps, to join us on the hill. Accordingly, Sandy Whillans, Walter Elliot and Robin Turner followed up some way behind us. Climbing between the two Glencoe groups, three of the Bangor party were carrying the casualty bag, ropes, and a searchlight.

We left Eric Moss and Taff Jones at base. Sandy and I each had a walkie-talkie. Due to the heavy icing on the steep sections of the path, the Bangor party, few of whom wore crampons, decided that it would be dangerous for them to continue, so I asked John Grieve, who was below me, if he could bring up the searchlight which they had been carrying. Dave Knowles didn't have crampons either but a spare pair was being taken up by Sandy's party who were only a short distance behind.

Alan and I reached the bottom of Crowberry Ridge and traversed to the foot of North Buttress, which is to the right of the ridge. Here, where we were temporarily out of the biting wind, we shouted upwards to try and locate the missing climbers.

'Hello there!' we called in unison at the top of our voices.

'Hello there!' Immediately we heard a call from high above. It was impossible to pinpoint but we knew that at least one of them was alive. We sat down on the iced rock and waited for John Grieve to join us. We were looking out across the dark expanse of the Rannoch Moor, fleetingly lit by the anaemic moonlight as dark clouds scudded across the sky. The lights of the Kings House winked invitingly 2,000 feet below and a dull glow in our rescue truck denoted the whereabouts of Eric Moss and Taff Jones. Beneath us, the penetrating pencil of light from the quartz-iodine searchlight stabbed the darkness. We flashed our headlamps to indicate our position to John; in a few minutes he was alongside us.

'Shine the light up Crowberry Gully, John,' I requested. 'We heard a call.'

'Aye, I heard it too,' he confirmed.

We still couldn't see anything, however, although once again we all heard a faint cry, 'Help ... Help ... '

'Let's traverse across the base of Crowberry Ridge and ascend Curved Ridge to see if we can locate them,' I suggested. 'We'll have more chance of locating them there, their calls will drift up on the wind.'

'That's a bloody good idea,' commented Alan, blowing his cold hands and adding with sarcasm, 'I always wanted to climb the Buachaille by moonlight.'

I told the other parties of this plan and suggested that they too should follow up Curved Ridge. Though it is not a difficult route, even when iced up on a winter's day, it can be an awkward proposition at night when carrying a heavy load. However, we had great faith in men like Walter Elliot, a shepherd who, had he been a mountaineer in the modern sense of the word, would have been outstanding. We knew they wouldn't come to any harm. Yet the Buachaille is a highly dangerous mountain under its winter mantle, as serious and technically demanding as many of the great mountains in other parts of the world. Snatches of a song drifted up from below, 'Why are we waiting? Why are we waiting?' One of the lower party must have hesitated for a minute on a difficult section and was being mocked by a fellow team member.

The three of us went on and as we climbed I thought of the close relationship we enjoy in our rescue team. There are no politics; if we need an item of equipment and have money in the funds, then we buy without recourse to a committee meeting or other formality. We never do any training as such; there are enough rescues to obviate this. The climbers in the team recognise the value of the shepherds and farmers – they know all the easy routes on the peaks and are all strong, reliable men. The shepherds and farmers, in their turn, appreciate their limitations in the technical climbing sphere and act accordingly, leaving the difficult climbing to the few of us who are experienced mountaineers.

The Buachaille rises in a perfect cone when viewed by those travelling westward across the Rannoch Moor on the A82; many of its ridges and gullies blend with one another near the rugged summit slopes. At the top of Curved Ridge, Crowberry Ridge and Curved Ridge merge into Crowberry Tower – a great block of rock like a medieval fortress; in the shadowy moonlight it reared up ghostlike in its winter apparel. We had to traverse across the east wall of this 'fortress' to gain the crest and top of Crowberry Ridge, which offered an exposed and steep 300-foot passage on unstable snow.

Wearily we kicked footholds across this steep section, facing into the slope and using our ice axes above us for added protection. We were comparatively sheltered at first but as soon as we gained the crest of Crowberry Ridge, directly under Crowberry Tower, we were assailed again by the biting wind –

the coldest we had felt for many a year. Immediately below us was the deep abyss of Crowberry Gully, which flanks the north side of Crowberry Ridge; there was a vertical drop down to the steeply inclined gully floor, several hundred feet below. We called down several times but our cries were thrown back at us, mockingly, by the wind. It was hopeless. Slowly we started to descend to the top of the ridge, where a slip would have meant a fall of more than 1,000 feet down vertical rock and steep snow and ice. However, we soon abandoned the attempt, which appeared extremely dangerous since we had no rope with us, and decided to await the arrival of our friends. We contacted them and learnt that they were then at the start of Curved Ridge. The three of us sheltered in the lee of some frozen boulders overlooking the Rannoch Wall, which, had it been light, would have afforded an uninterrupted view of the start of Curved Ridge. As it was, the lights of the lads appeared fleetingly like will-o'-the-wisps; occasionally we caught snatches of their cheerful conversation.

John Grieve, who is always bantering with Sandy, seized his opportunity and shouted down, 'Come along, you stupid policeman. You're not on your beat now, drinking endless stroupachs!'

'Get stuffed, Grieve,' was all that Sandy could retort, being somewhat out of breath.

There is always plenty of ribbing amongst team members on a rescue, and reminiscences of previous call-outs, especially when a rescue occurs in the same place as an earlier one; being on the spot again invariably refreshes one's memory.

'Did I ever tell you about the man who was hanged in his own sling?' I asked Alan, choosing the most gruesome accident in that particular neighbourhood, which had occurred a few years before.

'No, I didna hear that one, Hamish,' Alan rejoined as he settled himself more comfortably on some sharp rocks, temporarily upholstered by atmospheric icing.

'Well, let's hear about it,' said John impatiently. 'Another tale from the MacInnes "Chamber of Horrors"!'

'That should be Sandy's police cell,' argued Alan. 'It's full of bashed helmets – "blood-red crusted", to quote our great bard – and broken climbing ropes. It's a real climbers' morgue!'

'Aye, one's as bad as the other,' agreed John. 'Do you know that Willie calls Sandy and Hamish "Burke and Hare"? Every time a stag gets killed on the moor by a car they're on it for their rescue dogs like a flash.'

'Well, never mind,' I concluded. 'I see that you're not interested in furthering your knowledge of the local history of this area.'

'We didn't say that,' pointed out Alan, moving slightly as some ice melted and the full impact of a sharp edge of rock made its presence felt. 'Carry on, by all means.'

I told them how, one evening, we had received a call to say that two climbers had fallen down Crowberry Ridge into the lower section of Crowberry Gully; their fall had been witnessed by two companions who were climbing above. They had fallen in an awkward place and their friends, both good climbers, hadn't been able to reach one of the two – a girl. They did succeed, however, in descending the ridge and traversing round its base to reach the man who had been leading. They found him, hanging by his neck from a sling which had caught on a spike of rock; he was dead when they cut him down.

'I've seen myself carrying slings like that often enough' commented Alan at this point.

'We were very short-handed, I remember,' I continued. 'After a hell of a lot of trouble we got the girl on the stretcher from where she was lying, head first over a drop; I've no idea what prevented her from going over. Anyhow, to cut a long story short, we got her down, but by that time she was dead. All this was done when we had very little gear. Nowadays we would probably have taken her off using a cableway, and she would have survived.'

'Aye, it's a different kettle of fish now,' said John. 'We've got so much bloody equipment that it would take the British Army to carry it all up the hill at once.'

'Do you know,' said Alan, standing up, 'I wonder why I continue to climb. You blokes are enough to put anyone off!'

From time to time we were brought back to the world of reality by a message over the radio. On one such call we learned that Dave Knowles had joined forces with Sandy's party and that the remainder of the Bangor party had returned to Lagangarbh Hut for the night. Lights drew abreast of us across Easy Gully, which separates Curved Ridge from Crowberry Ridge, and we could now call to our friends quite easily.

'Follow our steps across the exposed traverse on Crowberry Tower,' I shouted.

Walter, with a casual 'okay', strode across them with his usual celerity, followed closely by the others. Alan shone the searchlight in their direction, bathing the snow in a brilliant white light. It was like watching a film show on a giant screen.

Presently they were with us on our exposed stance. There was Walter Elliot, Sandy Whillans, James Bolton – one of the Bangor party who possessed crampons and had accompanied this group – besides Robin Turner and Dave Knowles.

'As usual,' Sandy observed drily, taking out his ubiquitous pipe, 'you have to await the arrival of the experienced members with the ropes and victuals.'

'We should give you a bit more rope,' answered John, quick to take up the taunt. 'And you might hang yourself like the poor bastard MacInnes has just been telling us about!'

'Enough about the rope,' interrupted Alan. 'How about the victuals? I'm famished.'

We opened a few tins of self-heating malted milk and huddled in a group on a small ice ledge behind the frozen boulder.

Some ten minutes later, after we had consumed the malted milk, Alan started to uncoil 200 feet of rope to enable me to climb down the top section of Crowberry Ridge in search of the missing climbers. He belayed me as I climbed down the first 200 feet. It wasn't technically difficult but there was a lot of ice about and, unroped, any slip on this section would certainly have been fatal; however, with the rope I was safe enough. When I reached the end of the rope I tied it off on a spike and joined on another 200 feet of rope which I had taken with me, then continued the descent. From time to time I stopped and shouted and once or twice I heard replies, sometimes a whistle and sometimes a shout. It was still impossible to pinpoint them. Occasionally I dislodged a stone with my crampons which, after rolling a few feet, would hurtle off into space and continue for over 1,000 feet to the base of the gully.

I felt convinced that the shouts were from high up Crowberry Gully (for the missing party could easily have changed their plans and roped into the gully from the ridge). We had, of course, checked the bottom snow in the gully for steps, but found none. I inched my way down to the very end of the rope. By this time I was hanging on the steep wall which plunges into Crowberry Gully from the north side of the ridge. I was using a special locking clamp which moves only one way on the rope and on which you can hang quite safely. (I was to change my opinion of the safety of these devices shortly afterwards.) I had taken the precaution of putting a large knot on the end of the rope so that I couldn't fall off the end; then I paused and shouted for the last time, hoping to be able to determine the location of the answering shouts. This was not to be, though I heard another reply, from where I was hanging I couldn't tell if the shouts were coming from higher up or lower down the gully. So I spoke to John Grieve over the walkie-talkie.

'I'm afraid I still can't tell where they are. Have you had any luck up there?'

'Haven't heard a thing,' said John. 'Seems to be windier than ever now.'

There comes a point on a search, especially a dangerous search, when one must draw the line – a safety limit. I felt now that it was conclusively drawn for that night. We had gone beyond the bounds of justifiable risk, since dangers of exposure and loss of blood to injured climbers must always be balanced against dangers undergone by the team. Any further descent into the gully, which had a considerable amount of loose rock and overhanging sections not cemented with ice, would have been hazardous even in daylight. I turned again to the walkie-talkie.

'I'm coming back up now. I think we should abandon the attempt for the remainder of the night.' (This was not long since it was already almost 4 a.m.). Using the clamp I swiftly ascended to the top of the first rope and clipped this rope to my waist so that it hung behind me; after untying the bottom end of the other rope so that it could be pulled in from the top, I climbed up it to join the lads.

'There's only one thing to do: bivouac here for the night,' I said when I arrived.

'Bed and breakfast on the tower?' suggested Sandy.

'Yes,' added Walter. 'A snowy ledge and bloody malted milk!' As a final gesture Alan shouted down into the depths of the gully. In the brief silence which followed, someone thought they heard a faint shout.

'They're down there somewhere,' said Robin in a puzzled voice. 'But where?'

We cut out a small platform in the snow and ice on the flanks of Crowberry Tower, where some shelter was given by the edge of Crowberry Ridge, which jutted out to the north of us. Then we took off our crampons and stowed all our equipment on a small iced shelf. The bivouac tent consists of a large rectangular box with no bottom; it weighs only nine pounds, has four plastic windows and two sleeve ventilators, and can accommodate about ten people. We put the tent over us and squatted down on the cold ledge. I was fortunate to be near the centre at the back so that I could lean against the ice wall backing the ledge.

'You can see who the old hands at this game are!' commented Robin ruefully. He and James were in a most unfortunate position with their legs dangling over the edge and their bottoms on the slippery ledge. Below them – a long way below – was Easy Gully, and only the frozen seats of their trousers, the force of gravity and a numbed hold on the bivouac tent prevented them from plunging into its snowy depths.

'Ah, you apprentice rescuers have to go through the mill,' said Sandy. 'Besides, you'd better watch it or I'll give you your forty-fourth parking ticket.'

This called forth a hoot of laughter from the squatting audiences as Robin was notorious for collecting parking tickets and ignoring them.

Once we were settled, I contacted base again and asked if it would be possible for an RAF helicopter to be on standby in the morning. We then opened some more tins of the self-heating malted milk we had acquired as a present from an army captain whom we had rescued some years previously. The searchlight was burning continuously, giving heat as well as light in our frozen box. I was holding it when I happened to doze off for a few minutes; as my lap was the central table for goodies, the searchlight succeeded in melting a considerable amount of chocolate over my anorak – it even ran down into my boots. We soon learned also that the searchlight rucksack, which holds the battery, had been tilted at some stage and acid had leaked out. The acid had seeped through on to Alan Fyffe's down jacket and anorak; he now complained of a burning pain in the small of his back.

'At least your back's not cold!' observed John unsympathetically.

We began discussing possible plans for the morning. I picked up the radio and spoke to Willie Elliot, who was still at base.

'Willie, before first light in the morning could you and Huan climb to the summit by the easy route? I'll ask the helicopter pilot to drop two 600-foot ropes and some other equipment. Then you could both carry the gear down to Crowberry Tower, just above us.'

'Right,' said Willie. 'I got that.'

Up there at the bivouac we deliberated over the difficulties of the rescue. Had there been more snow in Crowberry Gully we would have had no hesitation in lowering an injured person down the steep bed of the gully. As it was, there was little snow and much ice, so a lower in the narrow sections would have been complicated. Besides there was the additional hazard of stone falls – it is almost impossible for a party descending a steep gully not to dislodge loose stones after the stretcher has been lowered a rope's length; these stones might easily cause further injury to the patient.

I certainly slept reasonably well that night, but I must admit I was in good training for such discomfort as I had experienced some particularly frigid bivouacs in the Caucasus that summer, during which all our party were frostbitten. This, I felt, was comparative luxury – I was probably in a fortunate position, for I know that Dave, Robin and Sandy spent a miserable night and Sandy looked quite exposed by first light. He had not taken an anorak with him, although he did have a down jacket; he was shivering violently and his face was drawn and drained of colour, like parchment. We sipped a few more tins of malted milk without comment, though some of us who had developed a violent dislike for it did not even manage to finish our meagre allocation.

We stood up and shook the ice off the bivvy tent; then stamped repeatedly on the ledge to try and encourage the circulation in our frozen feet. Our crampon bindings resisted our numbed fingers; they felt just like steel bands and it took ages to get the crampons fixed. After a cold bivouac you feel like a piece of rusted machinery. It is a particularly dangerous time in the day, for you are not entirely orientated and often feel unsteady on your legs when you first stand up. Usually bivouacs are situated in exposed places and this particular one was no exception. We were not roped because it would have been too complicated with so many of us. Moreover, the previous night, we had not been able to find a belay on which to secure ourselves.

I made contact with base, who informed us that the helicopter was expected at first light – about 9.30 a.m. We were no sooner organised, and considering going down the ridge below us, which leads to Crowberry Gully, than Dudley Knowles came on to the radio.

'Hello, Hamish; come in, please. Dud here.'

'Yes, Dud?' I replied.

'There's somebody wearing a fluorescent anorak, directly below where you're standing!'

For about five minutes he relayed detailed messages as I cross-examined him to try and fix the exact position of this figure.

'There's no doubt about it, Hamish,' he stated with finality, as I seemed slightly incredulous. 'It's a figure directly below where that person in the blue anorak is.'

This was John, standing at the every edge of the ridge where we had sheltered the previous night, below the frozen boulders. As I had descended 400 feet down this section the night before, it was hard to believe: I could only suppose that this climber was either unconscious or dead, as he – or she – had not responded to my shouts.

Across the lingering darkness of the Rannoch Moor we could hear the unmistakable drone of the helicopter, dead on time. We fixed the ropes again for the descent and asked Dud to suspend all previous plans: finding the climber in this unexpected location necessitated a replanning of the rescue operation, though we learnt that Willie and Huan had already left for the summit at first light as arranged. They could not be contacted immediately since they had not yet switched on their radio.

As soon as the ropes were uncoiled, I started down. The helicopter pilot had landed meanwhile and contacted me directly on the mountain-rescue radio frequency. I asked him if it would be possible to fly in close with the helicopter and give a definite indication of the location of the missing climbers. As he swept past (it was impossible for him to hover in such blustery winds) he guided me down; Dud also assisted me from base, using powerful binoculars. At the very end of the rope, some twenty feet from where I had been the previous night, I found the first climber: twenty-year-old Paul O'Hara – conscious and uninjured, apart from exposure. He was wearing a fluorescent anorak and was tied into the top of a small, rocky chimney.

'Are you all right?' I asked as I reached him.

'Yes, I'm okay,' he said, though his looks belied this: he was as pale as the snow.

'Didn't you hear me last night? I was down here at 3.30 a.m. this morning.'

'No, I didn't hear a thing,' Paul answered weakly.

I asked him whereabouts the girl was, though I could plainly see the rope which ran upwards from his waist, then led across and disappeared over the ridge about forty feet from us.

'Hilary fell up there somewhere,' he pointed. 'I had a fall earlier in the day and she took over the lead from me.'

'Hello, Hamish,' Dud interrupted on the radio. 'We can see another figure below you now, farther in towards the gully.'

'Yes, Dud,' I confirmed. 'I see her rope going down. I'll head that way in a minute.'

Without wasting any more time in talk, I worked my way across the face to where the rope dropped down over a vertical section. I knew that Paul would be safe for a few more minutes, tied into the rock chimney, and Alan Fyffe would be down shortly to put another rope on him and lead him back up to the others.

At first I couldn't see Hilary; she was more than 100 feet below me, down the vertical wall which was really a sidewall of a rock chimney, now partially filled with snow. I shouted down, hardly expecting that a reply would be forthcoming, for I was sure that she must be dead, either from injuries or exposure following the cold night.

'Down here,' came a somewhat feeble response to my calling.

I could hardly believe my ears and shouted back, 'Are you badly injured?'

'My leg seems to be broken,' she answered. 'I'm not too sure about anything else.'

'We'll be bringing help shortly,' I reassured her. 'I'll be about five minutes, organising things, before I can get a rope down to you.'

I contacted base and had a word with the helicopter pilot.

'Is there any chance of coming right in to the edge of Crowberry Gully, to winch Hilary up into the helicopter?'

'What's the approximate wind strength?' he countered.

'It's a bit difficult to judge,' I replied. 'But it must be close to force seven – blowing up the face.'

'Well, I'll take another trial run to see if it's feasible.'

'Okay,' I answered. 'If it's not possible to lift her off by helicopter, it'll be a very difficult evacuation because of the dangerous face below her present position.'

'Yes, I can appreciate that. It looks bloody awful, even from above. But don't hold out too much hope,' he added dubiously.

Belayed from above, using one of our ropes, I soon joined Hilary. She was lying on ice and frozen scree which formed the angled floor of a chimney. The chimney was about three feet wide, slightly overhanging on the ridge side; the opposite wall was only a few feet high and led on to a steep ledge of loose snow and rock. Hilary still wore her helmet and she looked in not too bad shape, though she was shivering violently. Her right leg was twisted in the most grotesque way, but somehow during the previous day, despite agonising pain, she had struggled into a plastic bivouac bag which she carried for emergency; this, coupled with the fact that the place where she lay was a natural shelter from the wind and snow, probably saved her life.

It is strange how ironical fate can be: one moment she was plunging down a vertical drop, the next she had landed in a perfectly sheltered cleft on this hostile mountain which is all too often merciless to its victims. She had survived this fall, which ninety-nine times out of a hundred would have been fatal. On 30 December 1970 it was a very cold night, even by Scottish standards:

below freezing point at road level. The temperature decreases, of course, the higher you climb; but it is wind which causes spectacular heat loss: the same amount of heat is lost by a body exposed to still air at 30 °C as one exposed to air at 18 °C in a 10 miles-per-hour (16.093 kilometres-per-hour) wind. That night, the chill factor on the high and windy ledges of Buachaille Etive Mor must have been exceptionally low, about -40 °C.

I gave Hilary some painkilling tablets but she was lying in such an awkward position that it would have been hopeless to try and move her on my own; there was little point, anyway, since there was not a better place to be seen. We both took some glucose tablets and I covered her up as best I could with the articles of clothing available. Meantime, Alan had come down and put a rope on Paul, who was now climbing slowly upwards.

When Willie and Huan contacted base, they were told of the change in plan due to the unexpected location of the climbers. I could only contact them through base because of reception difficulties so, via Eric Moss, I asked Willie to remain on the summit while we awaited word from the helicopter pilot. It was still possible that we could have the long ropes and equipment dropped off on the summit, and this would be the quickest way for us to get hold of them. I also mentioned that Robin and Dave would escort the rescued climber, Paul, up to the summit.

While I was relaying this message to Eric Moss, Willie and Huan had come down off the summit and taken a look down the icy descent route to the top of Crowberry Tower.

'I don't quite like the look of that,' remarked Huan.

'No,' agreed Willie. 'It's a wee bit steep!'

They were relieved when, a few minutes later, they heard from Eric that I had suggested they should stay where they were for the moment.

The helicopter made a series of passes close into the face, but, as we watched it, it was obvious that the attempt was hopeless. The air was far too turbulent. I wasn't in the least surprised when the pilot came on the air and reported.

'Hello, Hamish. I'm afraid it's no use. I just can't do it. The wind's too gusty to allow me to hold the helicopter in a hover. It's the worst possible wind in the circumstances. I'll return to the rescue truck now and continue the conversation from terra firma.'

'Fine,' I said.

When our interrupted conversation was resumed, I questioned him about the possibility of dropping a large quantity of ropes and pitons, either on the summit itself or near us.

'I can try' was his reply. 'But I can't even hover at the summit or close to where you are now – perhaps a bit lower down, near the bottom of Curved Ridge?'

'That'll do fine,' I answered, and immediately asked Taff Jones and Eric Moss to post someone to receive equipment at that point. Huan and Willie heard that we would abandon the summit equipment drop, so they took over from Dave Knowles and Robin Turner, who had arrived with Paul roped up between them. They came over the top of Buachaille Etive Mor with Paul to descend by the normal route. Robin and Dave returned to the scene of operations on Crowberry Ridge, passing Sandy, Walter, and James, who were remaining on their frozen ledge as link men for collecting equipment.

'Base to Hamish; base to Hamish. Come in, please,' Eric Moss was calling again. 'I'm afraid there's more bad news: the helicopter has broken down.'

'Sorry about this, Hamish,' the helicopter pilot came on. 'Hydraulic trouble, I'm afraid. I've been in touch with HQ and they're rushing up a mechanic right away; he's coming in another chopper.'

'Too bad,' I replied. 'It looks as if we'll have to resort to manpower again, but let me know when we can expect the other machine.'

'Wilco,' he said. 'And good luck, meantime.'

The party which had gone up the mountain to receive the equipment which was to be dropped by the helicopter was in sight now, but there was nothing to collect. This party included some of our rescue-team members – Wall Thompson, John Hardy and Dud Knowles – necessary men for the success of the whole operation. It was soon arranged that the other volunteers – mainly the Bangor University climbers – should carry the equipment from base and meet our chaps at the top of the Waterslab; they could continue together up Curved Ridge.

I had requested that this equipment, including the casualty bag, should be taken up to the halfway point on Curved Ridge, opposite the great rampart of the Rannoch Wall, which is a favourite playground for rock climbers in summer. Meanwhile, John Grieve had lowered the end of a rope down the wall, with a rucksack of rocks tied on to it to ensure that it would not snag. The equipment would be raised by means of this rope. We discovered that the casualty bag had fallen during our previous night's bivouac, so it was arranged that some of the Bangor party should retrieve it. I got in touch with base again to ask if there was anyone available – a climber preferably – to take the stretcher up to the bottom of North Buttress so that we could lower a rope there and haul it up later. Eric Moss came on the air.

'Got a chap, Hamish – one of the Creagh Dhu Mountaineering Club members. Hold on, I'll ask if he knows where to take it.' The precaution was superfluous, needless to say, as these lads are as familiar with the Buachaille as Eric is with his own boots!

'Hello, Hamish?' Eric returned. 'Yes, this chap here – Ian Nicholson – says he'll bring it up.'

'Thanks, Ian,' I replied, hoping that Ian would overhear. I knew him to be a leading rock climber and the task couldn't have been in better hands.

Alan Fyffe came down to join me on the ledge. Alan has a teaching degree but enjoys climbing so much that he now instructs mountaineering full-time. I first came to know him through Jim McArtney, who was killed on Ben Nevis the previous year with his girlfriend and another part-time member of our rescue team, Fergus Mitchell. Alan had come over the two previous winters to help me with my winter courses; he had been Jim's best friend. Together they had pioneered many of the hardest Cairngorm snow and ice climbs. As a partnership they presented quite a contrast: Jim, always the extrovert, laughing, ready to lend a hand anywhere; and Alan, a small compact, quiet man whose size belies his considerable stamina.

'How is she?' asked Alan.

'Remarkably good,' I rejoined. 'She's a lucky girl – aren't you, Hilary?'

Hilary smiled and answered, 'I guess I am!'

The trouble with such a complicated rescue is that it seems to take ages to get the lowering equipment assembled at the scene of the accident. It was now 3 p.m. and we still hadn't received all the necessary ropes and pegs. I heard over the radio that Donald Marshall, one of the Bangor party, had been hit in the face by a stone while he was climbing up to retrieve the casualty bag. The bag was now on its way up, and John Grieve, Sandy, Walter and James were busy hauling equipment up the Rannoch Wall. Over 2,000 feet of rope was now lying on the ridge above, and more first-aid equipment, since I only had a limited supply of dressings with me.

The relief helicopter arrived in under three hours. It did a quick run about 100 feet out from the face before it landed beside the other at the car park. The pilot came on the air after a few minutes.

'Hello, Hamish,' he greeted me. 'I've consulted with the other pilot and we agree that it's too risky to take the chopper into where you are – but we could perhaps pick up the girl from lower down if you can take her part of the way down by conventional means?'

'Yes,' I replied, 'that would certainly be a help, but I think it's going to take us a long time to lower her, even to the first possible pick-up point. It may take us until dusk. How long can you stay?'

There was a pause, then he replied, 'We have the mechanic with us and he thinks that he can get the other chopper repaired shortly and it will probably return to RAF Leuchars. I'll hold on here as long as possible, till about 4 p.m., if that's any use?'

'That would be terrific,' I said. 'I only hope that we can get Hilary down by then, but it is complicated. Anyway, I'll be in touch. Many thanks again.'

The lads above were now lowering ropes and equipment down to us. Sometime previously we had perfected a method of lowering by cableway which, as well as keeping the patient away from the face, with the stretcher slung horizontally, could also be used to take injured climbers off ledges where any normal form of rescue procedure would be very dangerous. I proposed to use such a cableway for this evacuation. However, we had no way of calculating the distance down to the bottom of North Buttress, directly below and slightly to the left of us; it was at least 500 feet, but was it more than this? We couldn't risk anyone going directly down in case there wasn't enough rope for him, and I didn't want to add a further rope to the main suspension rope as pulleys had to run on it and they would stick at the knot when Hilary was lowered.

I thought it might be necessary to use two separate cableways, one of about 500 feet, running in a line parallel with Crowberry Ridge; another, leading from the bottom of the first, across Crowberry Gully to the base of North Buttress. I asked Alan if he would go down on the end of the 600-foot rope, taking a line parallel with the ridge, on a climb known as Shelf Route which was pioneered in winter by Bill Murray, the well-known Scottish climbing author who is also the president of our rescue team. This ascent was later immortalised by Dr Tom Patey in his song, 'The ballad of Bill Murray':

> In that Tournament on Ice, Death or Glory was the price
> For those knights in shining armour long ago –
> You must forage for yourself on that ghastly Garick's Shelf
> With every handhold buried deep in snow.
> Murray did his Devil's Dance on each microscopic stance
> Recording his impressions of the view,
> There was green ice in the chimneys and black ice at the crux
> And not a single piton or a screw.

Dave Knowles belayed Alan, paying out the rope as he descended. Below, we could see that the stretcher had arrived at the bottom of North Buttress; Dud Knowles and the Bangor team had also reached this point.

Sandy, Walter, and James were still up on the exposed ledge on Crowberry Ridge. There was no shelter from the relentless fury of the wind, against which they were inadequately clad, although Sandy had somehow acquired a pair of windproof trousers. Undoubtedly they suffered the worst conditions of any of us, having to remain in the one spot. They couldn't move without using ropes and they couldn't escape from the arctic blast of the wind. But we needed them there – they were the only link which would enable us to get off our own ledge later, and I foresaw trouble even in this respect since time was getting on. One of the greatest hazards of Scottish winter climbing is the limited hours of daylight: about eight hours at that time of year. Not only must one be able to climb fast, but one must also be prepared, if unlucky enough to be caught out, to spend a very long night in cold conditions which are as severe, physically, as anywhere in the world. The damp cold in Scotland has a way of creeping into the very marrow of one's bones, and I have found it definitely worse in bad conditions than when climbing in the Himalaya in winter. James and Sandy were huddled in a corner of the ledge which looked over the Rannoch Wall. Sandy mentioned over his walkie-talkie that he was worried about James and, when I recalled how Sandy himself had looked that morning, I realised that we might easily have exposure cases on our hands if we weren't careful.

Alan had a walkie-talkie with him and used it to give instructions to Dave, who was paying out the rope.

'I'm down at the bottom of Crowberry Ridge now, Hamish,' reported Alan, his voice coming over in a series of crackles, interjected by messages now being passed between Braemar and Inverness police teams, who were engaged in a search in the Cairngorms. We even heard one of our friends, Kenny MacKenzie, who had been coming to help us on this rescue but was called up to the Cairngorms instead by his chief constable.

'Have you got enough rope to traverse into Crowberry Gully and get across to the bottom of North Buttress, Alan? We have about 140 feet left up here.'

'I don't know; I can try – I may just make it.'

Alan now changed direction, heading down and across into the gully, whose wall was overhanging at that point. The only way we could judge his progress was by the erratic jerks on the rope, for he was too busy to operate his radio. Five minutes later we were getting worried about him, for there was only about twenty feet of rope left. He came on the air again.

'I've made it!'

'Just as well,' I replied thankfully. 'There's no more rope! Try and clear the rope from the snags which happened when you changed direction, Alan.'

With assistance from the others, who had joined him, he pulled the rope taut and tried to flick it clear of the rock snags which had caused the rope to go down in a dog-leg bend so that it was useless, in the circumstances, for a cableway. This was what I had feared would happen. The only remedy was to send someone else down the rope to free it en route.

Wall Thompson was standing near me. He is one of the many people who could not stand the monotony of town life and grew so fond of Glencoe that he came to settle in the area. He obtained a timber-felling contract in a nearby forest, in partnership with John Hardy, another member of our team. Both are rock climbers of outstanding ability. Wall is a tall, strong, bearded man, abounding in energy. John, on the other hand, is slight and quiet. They always seem to be in a state of disorganisation – on this occasion Wall had no crampons – but this didn't deter him and he had climbed the mountain at speed and double-roped down to our ledge with great panache. He had taken a considerable risk in coming this far without crampons, for conditions were extremely difficult. He seemed a natural choice to sort the rope so that it hung in a direct line down to where Alan was standing – a small figure far below.

Dud Knowles and Ian Nicholson, who had arrived with the stretcher, were now beside Alan.

'Sure, I'll go down,' Wall readily agreed when I asked him. 'Where exactly do you want the rope?'

'Straight down to Alan at the bottom of North Buttress, from where we're standing now.'

'Right you are, then,' he answered, springing into action. He descended the wall in a series of great bounds, like a leaping kangaroo, using a figure-of-eight descendeur. In twenty minutes' time the rope was hanging free in the correct line and the party below started to tension it a little so that it hung away from the face.

I returned to Hilary, for I was not sure exactly what her injuries were – her foot seemed badly distorted and her leg was twisted at a strange angle. To complicate matters further, I couldn't really get in a position to attach properly a long splint which would prevent any movement of the hip and leg. While I was attempting this, Eric Moss came over the radio again.

'Base to Hamish; base to Hamish. Come in, please. Over.'

'Reading you loud and clear, Eric,' I said, picking up the walkie-talkie. 'What is it? Over.'

'There's an RAF doctor here who can perhaps give you any advice you may require.'

'Hello, doctor,' I called. 'It looks as if she's broken her thigh and there's something wrong with her hip – maybe dislocated. No other obvious injuries, plenty of bruising and cuts, her head is all right and helmet undamaged. Possible frostbite, though. We'll get her into the casualty bag in a few minutes. I've already given her two painkilling tablets – DF118. Should I give her any more, do you think, before I move her?'

'Is she still in pain?' he asked.

'Yes, she seems to be. She's had the pills over the last four hours.'

On the doctor's advice I gave her extra pills and finished off the splinting. Robin Turner had come down and helped to ease her up in order to place the triangular bandages under her leg.

'Helicopter to Hamish. Come in, please.'

My radio was lying in the snow some distance away so I went over to retrieve it.

'Reading you loud and clear,' I replied.

'I'm afraid we'll have to leave you now. It's growing dusk and we have to get back to base before darkness. Sorry we couldn't have been more help.'

'Many thanks for trying – too bad about the wind,' I answered. 'Have a good flight home. Out.'

'Hello there, Hamish,' called Eric over the radio. 'Alan has got the stretcher attached to the cableway at the bottom and it's ready to be pulled up the suspension rope.'

'Right. We'll do that presently.'

As soon as Hilary was put down and secured on the sloping ledge, we hauled the stretcher up on the other 600-foot rope. Attached to the stretcher was a large rucksack filled with items of first-aid, food, and about seven flasks of soup, tea and coffee. When at last we pulled the load up to our ledge, we couldn't partake of these refreshments; we were too exhausted and suffering from cramp; besides, it was now a race against time. A long, lingering shadow stretched out across Rannoch Moor – the shadow of the sentinel of the glen, Buachaille Etive Mor – and, across the valley, that of Sròn na Crèise lengthened imperceptibly. With the coming of darkness the frosty bite of the wind intensified as the first star appeared in the darkening sky.

We gave Hilary some coffee and lashed her to the stretcher in preparation for her aerial excursion. She showed considerable interest in what was going on – with good reason, since the drop below her seemed to fall away down to the Rannoch Moor, 2,000 feet below. The cableway was a prospect that even the most hardened climber might have jibbed at, and she must have felt particularly helpless, strapped on to the stretcher. As we finished tying her I told her what would happen; that the lower would be performed at speed and on no account was she to hold on to the suspension rope since her hands might get trapped in the pulleys. Just to be on the safe side, I enclosed her hands within the heavy casualty bag so that, even if she panicked, she would be unable to grasp the suspension rope.

Via base, we were in constant touch with the bottom cableway party; co-ordination during this phase was vital for, at a certain moment when the stretcher is lowered over the edge, clear of the rocks, the cableway rope has to be tensioned to keep the stretcher away from the face. At this moment the stretcher simply drops over the edge, so the timing must be exact for applying the tension.

John Grieve took the stretcher rope on the figure-of-eight lowering device while Dave and I were at the foot end of the stretcher, walking backwards towards the edge. Robin and John eased the stretcher down from the head end. Leading towards the edge of the cliff there was a steep and narrow broken ridge, about two feet wide, covered with loose snow. Dave and I worked our way to the extreme edge and then started to take the stretcher down vertically until the suspension rope would take the weight, once it was tensioned. Obviously, it couldn't be tensioned until it was over the edge as the rope would bear down on the stretcher; the suspension rope belay was at ledge level.

'Okay, Dave. Let it go,' I said. The stretcher dropped vertically, controlled from above by John.

'Tension, Alan,' I yelled over the radio.

'Tension,' Eric repeated over the police walkie-talkie, for the battery in Alan's radio had run down and he had to use another on a different frequency.

The suspension rope suddenly whipped into life as six strong climbers hauled on it from below. Hilary, who had been suspended vertically the second before, was hauled to a horizontal position in a trice. The slings on which the stretcher hung from the pulleys were so arranged that it would hang almost horizontally on the steep cableway. The stretcher heaved and, to anyone unaccustomed to this operation, it must have appeared that we were doing our utmost to dislodge the patient! She was, in fact, secure and perfectly safe at that moment.

'Let it go, John,' I shouted. 'As fast as possible.'

The rope shot through John's gloved hands and the stretcher sped down the cableway.

'Faster still,' I told him. 'She's a long way to go yet.'

The stretcher grew smaller and smaller as the rope ran out: 200 ... 300 ... 400 feet. Alan came on, through the base radio: 'Keep it going, Hamish. She's still a bit to go ... just now she's directly above Crowberry Gully.'

I could visualise the drop beneath the stretcher.

Back at base, Eric Moss held a microphone in each hand, one for each of the two radios, and was frantically relaying our messages. Unfortunately there were no other radios available and we were forced to operate on the different frequencies. We could scarcely see the stretcher in the gloom; just the glinting alloy of the headboard.

'Okay, hold it,' said Alan. 'We're releasing tension now.'

'Hold it, John,' I shouted.

John tightened his hold on the rope.

'Fine,' relayed Eric for Alan. 'Hold it there.'

'Down again, Hamish. We're lowering her on the suspension rope as well now, and she should land right at the foot of Crowberry Gully.'

'Wilco,' I replied, and shouted, 'lower slowly, John.'

'She's down now,' said Alan.

'That's great,' I told them. 'Thank goodness – I was a bit worried in case the suspension rope broke.'

The rope had been subjected to considerable strain during the lower for, as you can imagine, if a rope is suspended horizontally with a stretcher-load at its centre, the strain on it can be very great indeed. To give a simple example: if a one-ton weight were suspended from a tightly tensioned horizontal wire, so that the angle of the suspension wire at the point where the load was hanging was 160 degrees, due to the dead weight, then the strain on the suspension wire to each side of the hanging weight is three tons. The whole of our cableway suspension rope hung at an angle of almost sixty degrees, the rope was in poor shape, and it was subjected to about 500 pounds tension by the climbers. Such risks have to be taken on rescues, sometimes, when a further night out could perhaps be fatal for the injured and also the rescuers.

When Hilary landed safely she was examined by the RAF doctor, who, although no climber, had got this far in his shoes and everyday clothing. He found her in good spirits and full of her rapid descent.

'It was terrific!' she informed him.

We now began the evacuation from our ledge. A load of equipment had to be sent down the cableway so the 600-foot rope had to be raised once again. John Grieve had broken his crampons on the ascent the previous night, so he suggested that he should go down as well.

'Well, it's your neck,' I told him. 'There isn't a big safety factor, though we can leave the suspension rope fairly slack which will help a bit.'

'I'll risk it,' decided John. 'I don't fancy that climb up to Crowberry Ridge again.'

Indeed, we all knew that it wasn't going to be easy, for the wall above was vertical in places and the rope hanging down it had iced up now.

'Well, if you're going down, the other equipment will have to go down with you,' I added.

There were several hundred feet of spare rope on our ledge, as well as a great mound of pegs, karabiner clips, and pulleys.

'Hello, base; hello, base. Come in, please.'

'Reading you loud and clear, Hamish.'

'Can you tell Alan that John Grieve is coming down now on the cableway as his crampons have broken?'

Eric misunderstood this message and informed Alan that John had broken his glasses. Alan realised that this could be very serious for John as he can't see at all without them!

We slung two heavy rucksacks on to a pulley running on the suspension rope. John tied himself behind them on another pulley and the end of the 600-foot rope was tied to him. We lowered him over the edge, the cableway was tensioned slightly and he was lowered at high speed by Dave, who had taken over John's place at the lowering belay. Dave had also broken his crampon bindings on the ascent but felt that ascending to the summit was the lesser of the two evils! Anyhow, we hadn't sufficient time to do another lower that night for it was getting too dark. John took a walkie-talkie with him and gave us, as he put it, a running commentary on the trip. In a few minutes he was able to shout down to Alan. While he was hanging free, high above Crowberry Gully, he asked Alan to slacken off the suspension rope. As he was nearing the overhanging rock bounding North Buttress the suspension rope snagged against a section of rock, which fell away, narrowly missed him, and went crashing into the lower depths of the Gully. As soon as we heard that he had arrived, we dropped the ropes down the 600-foot face. It was then 5.45 p.m.

Earlier in the day I had asked for spare headlamp batteries to be sent up, but these never materialised and we were in a tricky situation, having only three headlamps – barely working on exhausted batteries – between all of us, including our three friends above. We had kept back two ropes on the ledge and I tied on to one of these and started to climb the chimney above me. This led on to the vertical wall. Though I have good night vision I couldn't see properly. I kept the rope, which still hung from above, running through a karabiner clip at my waist in case I slipped, but as it was coated with a film of ice it was extremely difficult to grip. I had, besides, hanging from my waist harness, a rope clamp which is designed for ascending: it has a spring-loaded cam which locks on the rope and should only travel in one direction, i.e. upwards. This was the type of clamp I had used the previous night. I did not use it at first on this section as I could climb faster and more simply picking my way up the snow-covered rocks than by dangling and ascending on a fixed rope.

When I reached the vertical wall I pushed the clamp ahead of me in case I slipped, but still put no weight on it. Suddenly, there were no holds left – if there were, I couldn't see them. After a particularly difficult move I was stranded on one small foothold with no handholds available, only the blank wall for balancing myself. I made a quick movement and slid the clamp up to the full extent on its sling; I had almost breathed a sigh of relief when I felt myself falling! I couldn't understand it, for the clamp cannot come off and the sling was still attached to my waist. The clamp itself must be slipping! Quickly I grabbed the rope and found myself back almost horizontally, pivoted on the foothold. With both hands I clutched the rope and, no doubt, fear lent me strength, for I managed to stop myself slipping, despite the icy coating. The boys below heard the sudden scrabbling of my crampons and shouted anxiously, 'Are you all right?'

'I am now,' I gasped as I began to climb the rope, hand over hand, and struggled up over the brink. My arms felt as though they had been stretched on a rack but I suffered no injury other than badly strained tendons which took several months to get better. I had gained a greater understanding of the shortcomings of certain rope clamps through this experience, but I might just as easily have finished my days instead at the base of North Buttress.

Two dark figures were silhouetted against the starry sky above me.

'What happened?' asked Walter.

'This bloody clamp slipped. I should probably have passed the stretcher party by this time if I hadn't managed to hold the rope!'

'Thank goodness you're up,' rejoined Sandy. 'We thought we were doomed to spend the rest of our days here.'

I looked past him and saw that James was still there, huddled in a ball behind a boulder.

'He doesn't seem too good,' said Sandy seriously. 'He's had about enough.'

'We've all had about enough,' echoed Walter, voicing everyone's thoughts.

The lads below tied the remaining rope to the end of the one I had trailed behind me and we hauled it up. I then threw the end of mine back down to them so that three ropes now led down to their ledge. They knew what to do and each tied on to a rope end. There was no belay at our ledge although the rope I had climbed was tied off higher up. But we were in too much of a hurry to bother trying to attach ourselves to it: we were all frozen through and could scarcely see by now.

It is in situations like these that accidents occur; the mind becomes numbed as well as the body. We felt a grave urgency to get off the mountain, for another night out might have been fatal for some of us. So we simply took in the ropes until they were taut to each of the lads; then they started to ascend, one behind the other. I was belaying John Hardy, who had no crampons; Walter was belaying Dave, and Sandy, Robin. They made good progress until they had reached, I judged, the base of the vertical wall. Then followed a pause; no weight was felt on the ropes. Suddenly, with a jerk, Walter catapulted forwards. I managed to take my left hand off my rope to prevent him from shooting over the edge; he regained his balance but was immediately jerked forward again. I felt more strain now on my rope and Sandy too was experiencing an alarming pull. All three of us were wearing crampons, which, fortunately, afforded some traction on our small ledge – two feet wide by six feet long, sloping down towards the drop.

There were shouts of alarm from below. The strain on my rope increased and I realised that John was leaning back and pulling himself up, hand over hand. When the weight eased off, I knew he was over the top of the steep wall below.

'What's the matter?' I yelled.

'Dave came off and landed on Robin,' he shouted back briefly. Dave and Robin arrived, exhausted, on the ledge. We were as grateful to see them as they were to see us. We all felt weak with relief. Though we still had to get up and off the mountain, I knew it well and, with the exception of a couple of places, it offered no serious problems.

We later learnt that Dave had fallen from directly above Robin and his cramponed foot had crashed down on to the small hold which Robin was grasping. Robin had a very lucky escape since the points of Dave's crampons bit in the gaps between his fingers and did not actually draw blood. After a brief pause, one foot anchored temporarily on Robin's hold, Dave had then fallen on Robin. This accounted for the double strain imposed on Walter and also the jerk which Sandy felt.

We had three headlamps between us. There was now a line of fixed ropes to the point where we had bivouacked the previous night. We started to ascend hand over hand, our joints and muscles protesting at the sudden, violent exercise. By the time we reached the top of the ridge, circulation was partially restored. Though there was no moon, there was a certain amount of starlight now we were clear of the shadowing flank of Crowberry Ridge. When we reached the bivouac spot we coiled up the ropes and cached them among the frozen boulders. We also left the searchlight and the bivouac tent.

'Do you think your mates could collect this stuff tomorrow, James?' I asked.

'Yes, we have a large party and some of them were resting today,' he answered readily.

I had requested Eric Moss on several occasions since 3.30 p.m. to try and arrange some form of lighting for us, since the Buachaille is not the easiest mountain to descend in darkness. There was evidently some misunderstanding about this, for he thought that Taff Tunnah, the team leader of the RAF Leuchars Mountain Rescue Team, would try and organise something with his own members.

We followed the steps that Dave and Robin had taken earlier that day with Paul. These led us across the face of Crowberry Tower, which we had traversed the previous night, then round the back of the tower and up a long snow gully towards the summit. John Hardy had collected his crampons at the bivouac site and now wore them, but as I ascended, using the headlamp, I cut steps up the steep, hard snow for Dave; any slip at this point would be disastrous; these snow slopes run down to the almost vertical drop of Waterslide Gully and down, over 1,000 feet below, to the heathery lower slopes of the mountain. We crossed just beneath the summit and carried on down the west side of the mountain to join the normal descent route, which overlooks Alasdair MacDonald's home, Altnafeadh.

We were both startled and relieved when the hillside was suddenly illuminated by a series of flares set off by the RAF party. In the corrie we were descending it was almost as bright as in daylight, but it was after 10 p.m. before we finally reached the road.

I suppose that during some other rescue on Crowberry Ridge, in the years to come, we will recall the night we bivouacked under Crowberry Tower. I have already heard Sandy reminiscing, 'You know, when I went up to Kings House bar that night and saw the lads having a few halves – for we understood that only Hamish, John, and Alan were going up the hill – I thought to myself, "Well, Whillans, you never know – you might possibly be up that ruddy hill tonight; you've seen it happen before." And, by God, I had second thoughts and said to Willie, "I'll just have a shandy instead!"'

6   Great Gully Avalanche

For climbers, the 1,200-foot-long Great Gully of Buachaille Etive Mor, Glencoe, is not a particularly attractive proposition. In summer it boasts of only one long waterfall pitch, while its upper regions are vegetated and uninteresting, high- angled scree and turf being more evident than rock. The climb starts from the lower slopes of the mountain and is contained within the walls of North and Great Gully buttresses.

In winter the gully has a different appeal. Should the snow conditions be hard, it affords a pleasant way to reach the summit. It has the further advantage of starting from a low access path and finishing at the very top of the peak.

In the summer months the gully is a natural water channel and, except during a long dry spell, a stream always cascades down its bed. In winter this stream freezes and it often resembles a small glacier. When a heavy fall of snow occurs, this ice offers little anchorage. However, the snow will usually consolidate and bond to the ice, unless followed by a thaw. But, if the snowfall has been heavy, climbers who are unaware of the ice beneath may break the surface tension and cause an avalanche.

Immediately after a snowfall there is an initial period of stability when the individual snow crystals interlock; this is followed by a period of instability. The rise in temperature during a thaw weakens the bonds between the crystals; should this rise in temperature continue, as it often does in close proximity to and under the influence of the relatively warm Atlantic Ocean, the crystals eventually become covered by a film of meltwater which acts as a lubricant and reduces the static friction. When this happens, the sheer strength of the snow is reduced to almost nil, and it is in such circumstances that wet-snow avalanches occur.

During a Scottish winter we can experience a very rapid rise in temperature, with prolonged warm spells. Under these circumstances a thaw may be so great that water percolates through the top layer of snow on to a harder layer underneath, often on to ice, as, for example, in Great Gully. It then runs down the surface of the ice, completely severing the bond between the fresh snow and the ice, so that the whole slope may be suspended for a critical period on its peripheral anchorages – the sides of the gully and, possibly, rocks which protrude through the ice.

Most avalanches occur during or just after a heavy snowfall. The weight of fresh snow is the most common of all the natural influences which increase the sheer stress in the underlayer of snow until it reaches its breaking point. During a heavy fall of snow, the stability of the snow cover will gradually reduce by this additional weight until the Stability Index drops below 1 and an avalanche begins. Obviously, steeper slopes will avalanche first, but avalanches from such slopes may be of only small magnitude. One point which many climbers do not fully appreciate is that steep and difficult gullies are actually safer during heavy snowfalls than the easier-angled ones, which, when they do avalanche, do so with a greater mass of snow. Slopes of around thirty to thirty-five degrees produce the most devastating avalanches which occur during heavy snowstorms. I am not, however, advocating that climbers in Scotland should go into the steeper gullies during a snowstorm!

In Glencoe, as well as having an information board for climbers which is used during the winter months to give prevailing climbing conditions, we also put up warning posters when there is acute danger of avalanches.

Conditions were terrible during one weekend in February 1970. Throughout the Saturday heavy snow had been falling which was both wet and sticky. Hamish Small, a climber from Glasgow, was with me in the house, for conditions were too bad for him to venture on the hills. About 3.30 p.m. Doris Elliot telephoned from Kings House Hotel.

'Hamish?'

'Yes, what is it, Doris?' – I recognised her voice.

'There's been an avalanche accident on the Buachaille – in Great Gully. Three people are buried.'

'I'll go up with the dogs immediately. Can you call out the team? Ian Clough is just back from Fort William. If you start with him we'll get things under way. Ask Dave Lambert – he's staying with him – to come up right away, would you?'

Dr Lambert was staying with Ian for a couple of weeks, recuperating from a fall he had had a few months previously. Now he was back climbing after a remarkable recovery and was going on the Annapurna south face expedition with Ian that spring.

Hamish Small had paused in his conversation with my wife Catherine – they realised that something was afoot.

'Quick,' I shouted as I burst into the room. 'An avalanche in Great Gully – possibly three buried. Hamish,' I added rapidly, 'will you dash out and grab Douglas Lang and Neill Quinn? I saw them arrive at the lay-by opposite a minute ago. Jeff Arklas, the youth hostel climbing instructor, is there too.'

'Right.' Hamish rushed out, leaving the door open.

In a matter of minutes, after throwing vital equipment into the back of the car, we headed up the road. The car swerved dangerously in the deep slush. A few stags were down at road level. The cloud was right down now and the

Glen had that forbidding look which it often assumes in bad weather. Dickens, when he visited Glencoe in 1841, thought that 'It resembled a burial ground of a race of giants'. It certainly looked like it that afternoon.

We slid to a halt at Altnafeadh. A few climbers were about and we quickly organised them to carry up necessary gear: oxygen, probes, alloy shovels and casualty bags. We had no sooner set off than Ian's party arrived, together with Douglas Lang and his friends. I spoke to Ian over a walkie-talkie.

'Hello, Ian. We don't know the full details yet, but it appears that there may be three buried in Great Gully. Can you take over base? It'll be essential to keep good contact with the main road in case we need more equipment. You may be able to keep casual helpers off the hill, too: we don't want to lose anyone.'

'Sure,' he replied. 'It's probably the best thing, in any case, as I've the flu coming on, I think.'

We had our two rescue dogs, Rangi and Tiki, with us; they jumped eagerly through the deep snow, anticipating work ahead. The path runs up from Lagangarbh, a small cottage now used by the Scottish Mountaineering Club as a climbing hut, rising gradually across the flank of the mountain until it intersects Great Gully, some way below the waterfall pitch. We met a group of climbers as we reached the gully.

'Where's the accident?' I asked.

'We're not sure,' a small bearded man replied. 'But we think it's up round the corner, below the iced-up waterfall.'

I asked Jeff Arklas if he would stay at this point to prevent any others following us up unless they were members of our rescue team.

'Yes, I'll do that, Hamish. I'll just let your own boys up, or any good climbers whom I happen to know. I don't think many will get past Ian, though,' he added.

'Fine, Jeff. Thanks.'

We put our crampons on, for it was obvious that there was thick green ice below the soft snow. Meanwhile, the dogs were rolling in the snow beside us.

A dog trained for avalanche rescue has the ability to find someone buried to depths of over ten feet, quickly. It does this by air scent, so no item of clothing is necessary. Working into the wind, the handler asks the dog to search the most likely area of the avalanche tip. It is of great advantage to know the point the person was avalanched from and also where he was last seen, since, if a line is projected down from these two points, he will most likely be buried in avalanche debris somewhere in the continuation of this line. The chances of finding him are proportional to the volume of debris.

There are other things, too, which the avalanche expert must consider. If the avalanche turns a corner in a gully, there is the possibility – in an avalanche of fairly dry snow – of the victim being carried to the outer edge of the flow and deposited there amongst the debris, for the speed of an avalanche is faster in the centre than at the edges. The lower sides of trees may trap and hold an avalanched man as the trunk breaks up the main force of the falling mass, leaving an eddy on the lower side. In high mountain regions, victims subjected to the destructive airborne avalanche can be hurled into the branches of trees. Such airborne avalanches can fall at speeds in excess of 300 miles per hour, and the pressure developed can exceed 22,000 pounds per square foot.

To date there is no faster method of locating a buried climber or skier than by avalanche dog. Different types of electronic equipment which have been developed – from CO_2 detectors to magnetic recorders – have all been more cumbersome, more expensive, and slower. The old technique of using probes is a reliable but slow method of search. This embodies two distinct types of search procedure: the fine probe and the coarse probe. The coarse probe, which is the fastest, has a seventy-six per cent chance of finding the victim alive – if the rescue party is on the scene right away. The fine probe, which entails insertions every eight square inches is, in theory, 100 per cent certain of finding the buried person, but it is necessarily very slow and there is little chance of finding them still alive.

We climbed up the gully to where the top surface had slipped away, leaving bare green ice. It was already 4.15 p.m. and it looked as if dusk was settling in.

I pressed on ahead of the others with the two dogs. At a point where the gully levelled off, below the waterfall, I saw several figures. There was about them the shocked look of those who had witnessed a tragedy. A man had just been pulled out of a hole in avalanche debris. Tiki went over to the prone figure; a girl who was standing beside him shouted and tried to drive the dog away.

'It's all right,' I called. 'The dog won't touch him. Just leave her.'

'How many are still buried?' I asked when I reached them.

'We're all out now,' a somewhat bedraggled man replied with a tremor in his voice. 'There were three of us under: Gunn, Fay and myself,' he added.

I knelt down beside the climber lying on the snow and felt for a pulse. Just then both Catherine and David arrived and I left the unconscious climber in the hands of the doctors. They cleaned the snow from his mouth and started to try to resuscitate him. In a few minutes Catherine asked Hamish Small, who had joined us, for the oxygen which he was carrying. We had only four minutes' supply and when this ran out, so did our hopes. But they continued with mouth-to-mouth and cardiac massage for fully fifteen minutes more. We were too late. Perhaps, if we had been on the spot a few minutes before, we might have saved him.

While the doctors were at work, I was trying to organise the evacuation. The other two avalanche victims – the girl and the chap I had been speaking to – were walking cases. There was a high avalanche risk where we were and I wanted to get everyone out of the gully just as quickly as possible. I had asked some climbers to put pitons in the gully wall beside the iced-up waterfall, and from these ropes now hung. The stretcher was already unfolded, ready for use.

Meanwhile, the male survivor – a short man, still with snow in his hair – told me what had happened.

His party had climbed the waterfall pitch and the leader of his group of three decided that the snow was too dangerous; they were in the process of escaping from the gully by the left wall when a party above them started an avalanche. This top party managed to survive the pressure of the falling snow, as one of them was well secured on to the rock and the others were held by the rope; but the avalanche quickly gained momentum and swept the lower party down the vertical drop, just as they were moving on to safer ground.

The leader was buried head first, about five feet down, in wet sticky snow with a very low air content. Fay Herriot, the girl, was to one side, buried head first as well, with her lower legs sticking out of the snow. The lad I was speaking to was buried under only a light covering and was out in a flash. The vertical height of their fall was about eighty feet but, fortunately, they had landed in a mass of soft, wet snow which had accumulated below. The girl was dug out by her companion in a few minutes; then they both scraped frantically with their bare hands to dig Gunn out.

Meanwhile, the climbers above, seeing the fate of the lower party, endeavoured to get down to them while one of them went to telephone for help.

Reluctantly the two doctors straightened up, exhausted after their efforts. They didn't like to admit defeat but they had done all they could. The Buachaille had taken another life. Probably more people have been killed on this mountain than on the notorious Eiger itself.

For a minute there was an uncanny silence, finally broken by my dog Rangi giving a bark. The dogs were getting impatient for I had them sitting in a safe section of the gully, in order that they could be used if a further avalanche descended.

I had now sent down all the people, including the survivors, who were not required for the evacuation of the climber. There were about twelve of us left beside the body. One of the Argyll police team members, Jim Brown, had come up with a 500-foot rope and this was soon tied to the rear of the stretcher.

'Hey, Douglas,' I laughed. 'Look at Jim Brown's crampon straps.'

'Good God,' said Douglas with glee. 'Binder twine!'

'Watch your language, laddie,' Big Jim admonished. 'You're awfully close to your maker up here!'

In one long run-out we lowered the stretcher right down to the path, where a large number of climbers were assembled. I had already reported to Ian over the walkie-talkie that the climber was dead and asked him to have an ambulance standing by. I spoke to him again.

'Hello, Ian. Hello, Ian. Come in, please.'

'Reading you loud and clear, Hamish.'

'We should be down in about one hour,' I continued. 'If you can ask the ambulance to be at a point directly opposite the gully on the main road, we'll come straight down and ford the river.'

'Wilco. Out.'

It was not until I was standing beside Ian, having a cup of coffee after the ambulance had departed, that I heard the sad news. Eric Moss came over to us.

'I'm sorry that it was a friend of both of you that was killed,' he began.

'What do you mean?' I asked in astonishment.

'The climber, Gunn Clark. Didn't you know him?'

'Gunn?' I replied, stunned. 'Surely not – I would have recognised him!'

'Good God!' voiced Ian incredulously.

There was no doubt about it, it was Gunn – a highly experienced climber, who some years previously, on a climb with the late Robin Smith, had made the first British ascent of the north face of the Grandes Jorasses, one day ahead of us. We hadn't seen them and thought that our party was making the first ascent. It wasn't until we met them in Courmayeur that we realised that we had been beaten to the route.

'What made him go climbing in such a place on a day like this?' asked Ian in a whisper.

'Yes, what made him?' I echoed. 'The conditions are unbelievably bad. Someone with Gunn's experience must have known that.'

Probably he had decided to get out when he discovered the vast amount of snow which was lying on the ice, but we felt that he must have known of this, even before he went near the gully.

'We will never know why he decided to risk it,' concluded Ian sadly.

7   Slab Avalanche

It was 2 a.m. when the telephone rang. As I staggered sleepily to answer it I knew there were two possible callers: the survivor of a mountaineering accident – or Tom Patey. Tom Patey was the general practitioner in Ullapool and was renowned – amongst other things – for his capacity to function on remarkably little sleep.

'Oh, hello, Hamish. Don't tell me I've got you out of bed?'

'No, no,' I assured him, grabbing an anorak which was hanging behind the door, for it was somewhat chilly. 'I always stand by for your calls from 2 a.m. onwards!'

'I think you've got it wrong,' he answered with a laugh. 'I can distinctly recall reading in one of my own articles how you call me at the most unholy hours.'

'The trouble with you,' I retorted, 'is that you've been out in the sticks too long.'

'I just thought I'd let you know – I'm always doing you unappreciated favours,' he said, 'that I know a good lad to instruct on your winter-climbing courses. His name is Jim McArtney.'

I had vaguely heard of Jim, one of the new 'tigers' of the Aberdeen school – Tom's old stamping ground.

'I don't think you'd find a better instructor anywhere,' Tom continued. 'He's a fantastic chap.'

'Tell him to come down to see me, Tom, and thanks! I'll probably see you in the north-west at the weekend.'

'You should try to get to bed a bit earlier,' he said as he rang off. 'You're not getting any younger!'

The phone went dead.

I had trouble getting back to sleep and thought over what Tom had said about Jim. Tom, not usually overenthusiastic about anyone's capabilities, must have been impressed with Jim. If anyone had a weak spot Tom would have pinpointed it within minutes and might, if the inclination took him, write a song about the unfortunate victim in an equally short space of time. This was never done maliciously, but with a mischievous genius that could be disconcerting.

Two weeks later I was in the Clachaig bar; a strongly built lad with a winning smile came over.

'You're Hamish MacInnes?' he began. 'Tom told me to look you up when I came down.'

'Jim McArtney?' I asked.

'Aye, the same.'

'Pleased to meet you, Jim' – shaking hands. 'Tom said you might be interested in helping with the winter courses?'

'Yes, I certainly would,' he replied, taking a deep gulp of the pint of 'heavy' he held in a large hand. 'When do they start?'

'Beginning of the year. Have you met Ian Clough who runs them with me? He's serving at the bar; come over and I'll introduce you.'

The three of us started work on the courses in January; as Tom had shrewdly predicted, Jim was a person in a thousand. Not only was he a mountaineer of extraordinary ability, but he was so thoughtful for others that nothing was too much trouble for him.

Two winters later Jim was still working with us. We should have held our annual search and rescue dog training course in December but, due to an outbreak of foot-and-mouth disease, this had to be postponed. It was held instead the following January.

Ian came up to join me in the Bidean corrie on the Monday of this course. I was with a large party of handlers and rescue experts from all over the country; we were simulating an avalanche and timing electronic equipment against the dogs.

'Good morning, Hamish.'

'Hi, Ian. Sandy here was just saying that you were coming up the slope like a halfwit – had a hard night?'

'The day I can't walk uphill faster than a Glencoe bobby, I'll hand my crampons to the scrapyard!' retorted Ian in his usual good-humoured way. He dropped his rucksack beside me and lit a Capstan.

'Do you know that Jim isn't back from Nevis?' he asked as he took a deep drag on the cigarette. 'He went up on Saturday with Mary Ann, John Grieve and Fergy.'

This caught my interest immediately, for I didn't know they had gone to the Ben. Mary Ann was Jim's girlfriend, a keen mountaineer in her own right and a singer and writer of ballads. John was a climber of wide experience, while Fergus Mitchell, the other member of their party was a truck driver who spent long vacations in Glencoe – when he had enough money saved – and was, like Jim and John, a part-time member of our rescue team.

'What climb are they on?' I asked.

'One of the big routes, I think.'

'But none of those should have taken them more than eight hours or so,' I protested. 'Unless,' I added, 'Fergy's arm gave trouble.'

'Doesn't it dislocate?' Sandy interjected.

'Yes, that's one of the reasons why we can't have him instructing on our courses,' I replied.

'Come to think of it,' said Ian, 'that's probably what happened – and I bet they forgot to take headlamps!'

'We'll be able to kid them about this for the next few years,' I chuckled. 'I can just hear Jim saying to his course members, "Now dinna forget your head-lamps, chaps – you never know when you may be held up on the mountain".'

Apparently, word had come to the police station from Kinlochleven School, where John Grieve was then teaching, that John hadn't appeared for the morning classes. Kenny MacKenzie, the police constable at Kinlochleven, was alarmed and contacted his Fort William station instantly. A small party of Lochaber Mountain Rescue Team then decided to go up to Ben Nevis, with a few of the police team, to see if they could contact the missing party.

One of Sandy's police constables came over to where we were standing.

'A message from the Fort William police, Hamish. They've seen a solitary figure high on the Tower Ridge.'

'That's strange, isn't it, Ian? I wonder if they've left Fergy to go down for help?'

'Surely one of them would have stayed with him?' he mused, stamping his cigarette into the snow.

'I don't like it,' I stated. 'There's something strange about this.'

'I'm thinking of the thaw that's started now,' said Sandy with emphasis, drawing on his pipe.

'Oh, the lads surely wouldn't get caught with that' I answered, but a doubt remained in my mind. I added, more to put my own mind at rest, 'They know enough about snow structure and avalanches. Jim, at least, has been to dozens of our lectures on the subject.'

'Remember that rapid rise in temperature yesterday?' Ian recollected. 'It certainly was dramatic.' We had been digging graves in the snow for 'victims' for the dogs to locate. In a matter of minutes the snow was running with water as the wind changed from the east to a damp, warm south-westerly.

As we stood there, some twenty men were spread out across the large snow slope above us, all with probes poised, ready to start searching for a buried man as part of the exercise. Eric Langmuir, a colleague of mine and an expert on snow avalanches, was combing the adjacent area with a small electronic instrument: one of the buried men carried a minute transmitter unit, a new device designed for skiers and rescue-team members. All these operations were being timed by stopwatch by John Huxley, of the Countryside Commission.

The policeman's walkie-talkie came to life.

'Hello, police one; hello, police one. Come in, please.'

'Reading you loud and clear,' the young constable replied.

'A further message for Mr MacInnes. Can he proceed to Fort William as soon as possible? A helicopter will land in Glencoe in half an hour to pick him up. Cries for help have been heard from a figure on Tower Ridge. Over.'

'Hello, base. Police one here; received that message. Hamish MacInnes and Ian Clough have heard your message and they've just left. Out.'

The constable had probably never seen two people move so quickly on the hill before. As we dashed down the hillside, grabbing our packs, I had just enough time to shout to Sandy, 'Can you look after the avalanche exercise? We'll be in touch as soon as possible.'

I will never forget running down that path. Though I call it a path it is really quite a steep route, crossing several small rock faces. There was still a fair amount of ice on the hill, yet we didn't slacken speed. In about fourteen minutes we had descended over 2,000 feet from the corrie and arrived, breathless, at the main road.

A policeman came over to us, clutching a walkie-talkie.

'It's too windy for the chopper to land, lads. You'll have to go to Fort William.'

'Ian, I'll see you at your house in a quarter of an hour,' I said, as I gulped lungfuls of air. 'I'll pick up my car – it's faster – and collect some more rescue gear.'

'Right,' he replied, dashing off to his van.

We hurtled through Ballachulish at a breakneck speed and skidded to a halt at the head of the queue for the Ballachulish ferry. The ferryman, realising that trouble was afoot by the blast on the horns, returned from the other side at once; we were swiftly carried to the north shore and soon on our way along the thirteen-mile stretch of the twisty A82 to Fort William. The particular car I had then – a Jaguar E-Type – developed some 300 brake horsepower in its modified state, and this was put to full advantage on the road – but to no avail. When we arrived at the helicopter landing ground we were told by the police that the machine was grounded by wind at Connel, near Oban, where it had flown for refuelling. We felt frustrated.

'Can I have a word with the pilot?' I asked the police sergeant.

'Aye, but you'll have to come to the station to phone.'

'Right then.'

It took about four minutes to contact the pilot.

'Hello there,' I said. 'This is Hamish MacInnes speaking from Fort William. I understand that there is some difficulty in taking your machine up here?'

'Yes, I'm sorry we couldn't pick you up in Glencoe but it's gusting to force nine and I'm not supposed to fly in such conditions.'

'Well, it's most urgent that some of us get up the mountain right away. We feel the situation is extremely serious and it could save us valuable time.'

'I guess I'll give it a go, then. But don't rely on me – I may not make it.'

'Any luck?' asked the sergeant from over the other side of the table.

'He's going to try,' I replied. 'I suppose I should get back to the landing field. Is there any further word from the Lochaber boys on the Ben?' I jerked my thumb at the base station radio, crackling in the corner of the room.

'Nothing new. Just the one person on the side of Tower Ridge. Ian Sutherland, the deputy team leader, is trying to get to him now.'

'Is Arthur Hill there too?' I asked. Arthur was then the leader of the Lochaber Mountain Rescue Team.

'Yes, he's at the hut, coordinating things. They're also searching the base of some of the climbs.'

'Well,' I called as I went to the door. 'I'll be in touch in due course.'

'Oh, before you go,' he said, 'if the helicopter can make a second trip up, I'd like one of my constables to go – Angus MacDonald. You remember him? He was on one of your courses.'

'Sure, I remember Angus; your Highland Games expert. There may also be one other from our Glencoe team here by then.'

At the landing field – actually the town football pitch – I joined Ian. With him was John Grey, one of our team.

'Any luck?' asked Ian.

'He's going to try it. Should be here in about fifteen minutes if he's coming at all. The wind's bad.'

There was a great throng of people about now, as well as many press photographers. Someone shouted, 'I can hear a helicopter'.

Sure enough, the traction-engine-like note of the machine could be heard, coming up Loch Linnhe. As it landed I shouted to John, 'Can you go up with Angus MacDonald? That's him over there.' I pointed to Angus's athletic form; he was wearing the police-issue red anorak.

'Aye, I know Angus,' said John. 'Will I take the searchlight?'

'Yes, do that,' I said.

'Well, we'd better go,' Ian shouted above the din made by the settling Whirlwind Mk II, 'if he'll take us!'

Bending low, but keeping well within the vision of the pilot, we raced over to where the helicopter had landed. The winch man took our packs. He also gave me a headset so that I could speak to the pilot.

'Pilot here, Hamish,' came over the radio after I had introduced myself. 'We got here all right, but don't know if we'll get much farther: flying conditions are very treacherous. These machines are like bricks in certain conditions.'

'Well, even if you can get us part of the way up, it'll be a help,' I shouted, for I was still being deafened by the roar of the engine.

'Ready?'

'Yes,' I replied. 'Whenever you are. There are two more to go up next trip if you can manage it.'

'We'll give it a go.'

It was like being inside a punchbag which was being pummelled by an invisible fist. One moment we were climbing steadily, the next we were slammed down at alarming speed. Slowly and fitfully we gained height above the aluminium works, then followed the pipelines which come down the flank of Ben Nevis and feed the turbines at the factory. We travelled east for a while and were soon approaching the Allt a' Mhuilinn glen. We were no longer buffeted by the wind – instead, a steady and persistent pressure of wind weighed upon us, as it whistled down from the corrie above. Ben Nevis looked grim. The origin of its name is shrouded in history, but that day the interpretation 'the Venomous One' seemed singularly appropriate. Directly ahead of us in the valley we saw the Càrn Mòr Dearg Arête, a slender neck of ice and rock connecting Ben Nevis to Càrn Mòr Dearg; beyond this arête lies Glen Nevis. A bard of an earlier age must have thought little of this pleasant glen, for he wrote, 'A glen on which God has turned his back: the slop-pail of the great world.'

I was almost mesmerised, watching the ground creep slowly past, when suddenly I realised that we were making no headway. I had seen the same snow-covered boulder for a full three minutes.

'It's no use, Hamish,' the pilot came on. 'Can you jump out? I'm having trouble holding it'

'Right,' I called. 'Many thanks.'

I gave the headphones to the winch man, grabbed my rucksack and motioned to Ian. We watched for the signal from the pilot. He gave me a thumbs-up sign: we were still some fifteen feet above the ground when I jumped into the snow-covered slope. A second later, a thud, and Ian was beside me. In an instant the helicopter had vanished. It was plucked, like a piece of chaff into the gale as it headed back to Fort William.

'Well, that was an experience,' said Ian, shaking the snow off himself. 'But I'm glad I don't have to travel to Fort William with you by car, or by helicopter up Ben Nevis, every day. I've aged five years in an hour and a half!'

We set a fast pace to the hut as we were travelling light. In the past I had trod this path with Ian on several rescues – none were to be as tragic as this occasion. When we had travelled some way up the well-beaten trail through the snow we heard the helicopter returning below us. It was John Grey and Angus being ferried up. On the return trip of our flight the pilot had lost the doors in a particularly violent gust.

The climbing hut below the north-east cliff of Ben Nevis is a squat, dwarf-like affair, offering only limited resistance to the harrowing wind, and built like a medieval castle, even to the barred windows. Arthur Hill had just returned there from a quick search of the base of Tower Ridge.

'Hello, Arthur,' I greeted him. 'Seen anything new?'

'Not a thing, Hamish. I'm worried.'

'It certainly is strange,' agreed Ian as he took off his rucksack. 'I don't suppose there's anything further been heard from the man up top?'

'Not yet,' replied Arthur. 'You can see the figure from here, even without binoculars – see? Just right of the tower.'

We followed the line of his outstretched arm and could discern a red dot high up the ridge.

'We'll just have to wait until Ian Sutherland gets to him,' said Arthur. 'Let's go in and have a brew.'

We had some tea and John and Angus arrived. Behind them a steady stream of climbers came up the path. It had been announced on the six o'clock news that expert help was urgently needed. The switchboard in the police station was jammed by incoming calls; climbers were volunteering their assistance from all over the country. Now a rigorous control was being set up to restrain the good intentions of these climbers unless they had been personally vetted by one of the Lochaber rescue team.

It was growing dusk.

'I hope we hear soon,' muttered Ian. 'It's going to be difficult if we have to climb Tower Ridge or one of the other routes in the dark.'

'It certainly is,' I agreed. 'Remember the last time we climbed the ridge on a rescue? That was in 1958, I think.'

'Was that when the three were killed in Zero Gully?' asked Arthur.

'Aye, that's right,' confirmed Ian. 'I was with the RAF Kinloss Rescue Team then. I was spending the weekend climbing with Hamish.'

'It still makes my stomach turn, thinking about that accident,' I said. 'Their balaclavas were filled with their brains.'

'Hello, ridge party. Anything to report?' A team operator sitting at the table reiterated this appeal at ten-second intervals to Ian Sutherland's party.

'We'll soon be there,' Ian came back loud and clear. 'It's a bit awkward where we are at present.'

Moments later his voice reached us again. 'It's John Grieve who's up here. I've just spotted him. Hold on a minute … '

What actually occurred on the windswept ridge that weekend in February is best described by the survivor, John Grieve. With remarkable stamina he survived when many would have succumbed to the extreme mental and physical strain. The prevailing wet conditions were probably the worst possible under which to endure this kind of exposure. This is John's account:

> Three of us left the hut halfway up Nevis fairly early in the morning. The original intention was that Jim and I were going to try and climb Point Five Gully that day, but the conditions weren't particularly favourable for such a major climb. Instead, we decided we would split into two ropes and climb as a party of

four with Mary Ann and Fergy Mitchell, on the Italian climb which is on the Tower Ridge of Ben Nevis – a route which is hard but comparatively easier than Point Five Gully.

It was cold when we reached the hut, with a very low mist. We decided when we reached the bottom of the climb that conditions were quite safe – the climb was in very good condition – so we would carry on. McArtney and I climbed together to start with, followed by Fergy and Mary Ann. The main difficulties of the climb are in the first 300 feet: the snow was excellent and we climbed at quite a fast pace, which left us with an easy section to the crest of Tower Ridge. This section was about 600 feet of reasonably easy snow climbing.

We decided, as it was still early in the day, that we would head across on a diagonal line to give ourselves a longer climb – a more difficult climb – to finish the day off. Because of the very high winds, there was a tremendous amount of new snow deposited here which had not been apparent before; it had accumulated in the lee of the ridge.

We had just finished ascending a difficult pitch which was not on the route, it was on unexplored territory – Jim had led it. I was still at the bottom of this and the other two had climbed up to Jim. Then it was my turn. We continued on this upper section which had, as I mentioned, a large concentration of snow. During this period there was a very remarkable rise in temperature which wasn't apparent to us at the time. The wind was very high – a tremendous wind – and the cooling effect of this wind belied the temperature rise. It was after this difficult pitch that the tragedy occurred. The other three were round a corner; I was still last man, being belayed by Fergy. Jim, I assume, was in front at the time because we were all roped together.

The climb continued from this point, round a corner, skirting an overhanging rock on to a large snow basin which led easily to the crest of the ridge and the end of the route. The rope, which had been tied to my waist, had jammed lower down. The wind had blown it out into the face and I had to move round the corner. The easiest way to unsnag the rope was to untie it from my waist; I was in the process of flicking the rope round a spike of ice-encrusted rock when there was a roar. This is the thing I remember most vividly – a loud roar. It was very difficult to think what was happening. In these sort of situations you react instinctively. Straightaway I cowered underneath the rock overhang, dug my ice axe in, and just waited until the holocaust subsided.

It's difficult to describe your reaction at the time, because you're so mixed up with great feelings of grief when you realise what's happened. It takes a long time to appreciate what has actually taken place. Then comes the indescribable sense of relief which is present with most survivors, though they don't often admit to it. One of the first emotions is the realisation that you're still alive, albeit in a very dangerous situation – you are still alive.

Then you start thinking – what has happened? Everything's quiet. There was still, dust-powdered snow in the air and an ominous silence, for the wind had suddenly dropped. The first thing I did was to shout. I shouted, 'Jim, Jim.' I wasn't expecting an answer, but it was the one thing I had to do. I had to take stock of the situation and find out exactly what happened: you can't quite comprehend it, even although you know, deep down, that three people have just been killed and you are left there alone. Then you somehow push all these things aside. They become something that you think about later; it's got to be faced in the future. For the moment you've got to get yourself out of your immediate predicament.

I was still a few hundred feet from the top and I didn't really know what was in front. It was misty. The wind had got up again, so I went round the corner; what had been a large basin of snow was now a vast, smooth sheet, perhaps 200 feet high, of very hard-packed snow. I climbed up this, then crossed to the side until I came to a big slab break-off.

The avalanche break-off was three or four feet deep, perhaps 100 feet wide and 150 feet long. The whole section had slid – hundreds of tons of soft slab had slipped off the harder layer underneath, taking with it the three climbers; there was no way they could have tied themselves to the mountain that could have stopped this momentous force which hurtled them 1,000 feet down the face.

In a situation like this you become concerned for yourself; you've got to get out of it, unaided. My first thought was of the snow above, which was no longer supported by anything below. It was, in fact, a suspended layer, perhaps ready to fall down again.[1] I traversed across to the left, against the rock where the snow wasn't so deep and I knew I could get secure handholds on the rock. I carried on in this way to the summit of the ridge.

---

1. In fact, this is invariably safe.

Once on the ridge I found there was a blizzard blowing and it was growing dark. That night I spent a lot of time trying to get up or trying to get down, but mostly I sat thinking. This was the worst part: the most difficult thing was to comprehend what had happened. My first reaction was, 'This is it, this is me finished. If ever I get down, climbing will be a thing of the past.' There had been other accidents, other friends had been killed before, but here were three people and one a girl ... One of them, McArtney – a particularly close friend; perhaps one of the most cheerful people anybody would ever want to meet. He was full of life, a tremendous companion and liked by everybody. This is said about a lot of people, but it was really true in Jim's case; it was perhaps my greatest sense of loss.

Then the more practical things came to mind: 'What are you going to say when you meet his parents? What's going to happen when you see his sister?' These are the things that start preying on your mind. These worry you more than anything else. These thoughts filled the night for me – it was my biggest nightmare, thinking all these things.

Dawn came and a day passed. Late the next night, when Ian and some friends of mine of the rescue team arrived, I put these things out of my mind and I got down. Then the whole thing snowballed ... a lot of things happened ... people to meet ... reporters to speak to ... funerals to attend ... all those chores which absorb you for a while. It's later that you have to come to terms with yourself: whether you will in fact climb again. But it's a personal thing and you have to come to terms eventually. Some people call you callous, some people accept it – knowing it's a terrible waste of life but that climbing is something you just can't stop doing ...

When we had discovered that the party had been on the Italian climb, Ian and I, together with a small party of the Lochaber team and the police, set off for the bottom of the route. Andy Nichol, one of our dog handlers and a member of the local team, came too with his rescue dog.

'Have you ever seen a thaw like this, Ian? The snow's just running with water. We'll be lucky if we're not avalanched too.'

'That great snow slope up there under the tower worries me,' said Ian. His knowledge of Ben Nevis was vast, gained through many years of climbing on these dark cliffs and icy gullies. I knew what he meant – a great open snow slope, to the right of the avalanche which had taken the others down, was even then possibly hanging on its last weakening peripheral anchor. A certain amount of water helps to bond snow, but as the moisture increases the molecules tend to slide apart – as in slush – and snow resting on a harder underlayer is liable to slide, for the meltwater runs down this hard underlayer and severs the bond.

'Well, as the Karakoram porters say, "Insh-Allah", I laughed. We were in the lee of the face now and out of the wind, so we could speak quite normally. Fate spared us that night, but Ian was to meet his death shortly after this when an ice sérac broke off during the last few hours of the Annapurna south face expedition in the Himalaya.

The snow slope steepened as we drew near the base of the climb: an icy funnel rising almost vertically into the great sweep of rock above. I could now pick out the snow-swept ice of the first pitch with the beam of my headlamp, which wheeled round as I scanned the face.

'We'd better spread out now,' I suggested to Ian; the others were still some way behind.

'I'll take the right-hand side,' he replied.

We moved up slowly, combing minutely every inch of the gleaming white slope. Presently we came across avalanche debris.

'Looks pretty recent this, Ian; bloody hard compared with the rest of the slush.'

'This is about the spot,' Ian shouted back from the other side of the avalanche tip.

Just then I spotted a plastic bag and, beyond it, an inch of red-coloured rope sticking through the surface.

'They're here,' I yelled. The rest of the party had now caught up with us. 'They're buried here. Let's have the dog and the spades up, Andy.'

'I'm here,' Andy gasped breathlessly. 'Don't know if it's much use trying the dog, it's so wet – there can't be any scent in this stuff; it's packed in like half-set cement – but we may as well try.' The dog did in fact indicate all about this spot.

'Let's get digging,' said Ian. 'They're here all right.' Using a probe we detected several buried bodies, some quite deep, and soon we were digging like mad while all the time, in the back of our minds, was the thought of the poised slope above.

'How about standing over on those rocks there with your dog, Andy, just in case we get a shower of snow?'

'Aye, all right, Hamish. My back's about broken with this digging anyhow. I can hardly credit that this snow could be so hard when everywhere else it's slush.'

'That's the effect of high pressure coming through the narrow defile above,' I said. 'The snow freezes solid as soon as the pressure is released.'

It took us about an hour to dig down to the first of our three friends. I always think with horror of the dark nights when I have had to dig for buried climbers, sometimes very close friends. It is the uncertainty, the macabre exhumation, and always there remains the question, 'Can he still be alive?' Once he's uncovered you must make sure and may have to clear his airway to attempt resuscitation if there is any hope at all.

There was 450 feet of climbing rope tied to the three climbers. This now criss-crossed through the snow, frozen as hard as reinforcing rods, and hampered our excavations. We were soon dripping with sweat. In our hearts we knew that no one could have survived such a fall and burial; they had now been buried for twenty-four hours. Very little air was trapped in this avalanche because it had fallen down such a steep face that few snow boulders – between which air is sometimes trapped – had formed, as would probably have occurred on an easier-angled slope. By 3 a.m. we had uncovered the last person – Jim buried head first deep down in the avalanche tip. We knew from their injuries that they must have died instantly.

Ian and I looked silently down on our three friends in the illumination of our searchlights. We probably knew all three better than we knew our own families. I thought of Tom Patey, who was coming down to Glencoe that night. I had forgotten to leave a message for him.

'I suppose that Tom will be on his way up,' I said to Ian, in the hush which had ensued as we laid the corpses out, side by side. By this time the searchlights were becoming dim and we were all exhausted.

'I think we should leave them all here until first light,' I said. 'What do you think, Arthur?'

'Good idea,' he answered. 'The sooner we leave here, the safer for us all.'

'Okay, lads. Let's get back.'

We left one stretcher beside the bodies and trudged back in knee-deep slush. Below us, down the full length of the glen were strings of lights. Climbers were still coming up in their dozens but, finding it impossible to get into the hut, were told to return. Somehow or other they had evaded the selection party below.

There were over seventy people inside the hut, many our friends: Tom Patey, John Cunningham, Fred Harper, and numerous other ace climbers. It was almost impossible to move. We told them that we were leaving the bodies until the morning and that only a few people would be needed to carry them down. John Grieve came in, looking remarkably fit after his gruelling experience. Ian Sutherland said afterwards that he had climbed down with amazing competence for someone exposed so long on the mountain. He carried on down to Fort William after a hot drink.

Most of our team members were also in the hut. Sandy decided to go back down with Willie Elliot, Tom, Huan Findlay and the rest of our group. I stayed with John Cunningham, Fred Harper and a handful of the Lochaber team, in order to take the corpses to a point where the helicopter might be able to land the next day. Ian went down with the others to organise our climbing courses.

The floor of the hut was awash with melted snow; the atmosphere oppressive and steamy, like the inside of a laundry. None of us slept much that night. There were still about thirty-five of us in a hut designed to sleep thirteen; the air was laden with moisture. As the light filtered through the barred windows, we stirred; a thoughtful policeman made breakfast for those of us who were to recover the bodies. We struggled into our soaking clothes.

Retracing our steps of the previous night, we soon arrived. We placed the bodies on three stretchers and lowered them down the gully below the climb. By midday we were all back at the hut. The RAF men informed us that a helicopter would come up to a point about half a mile below the hut. We loaded the bodies and I flew down with them; I had to get back because it was the last day of the dog course.

Tom was waiting at the landing field.

'Jim's father is here,' he said in a strangled voice as I struggled towards him through the crowd. 'He wants to discuss the funeral. Jim's to be cremated in Aberdeen.'

'It's just beginning to dawn on me now – the appalling tragedy of this, Tom,' I said. 'I can hardly credit it.'

'It's bloody shattering,' answered Tom, not usually given to invective.

'How could a chap like Jim get killed in such a way?'

'Jim's father wants one of us to read the service,' Tom continued. 'I can't do it – will you?'

I thought for a couple of minutes. 'No, I can't, Tom. You knew him longer than I did. It would be really appreciated if you did it.'

Just then a stocky man with glasses came over – Jim's father I discovered later. He was quite unlike Jim except in temperament. In this small man was the same quality of magnetism that was so marked in his son. Later, when I came to know Mr McArtney, I developed a great respect for him and his beliefs: he had a sane and balanced outlook in life and, though a communist like Jim, he didn't try to impose his views upon others and, indeed, seldom spoke of politics unless asked for an opinion.

'This is Jim's father, Hamish.'

'How are you, Hamish?' his firm hand clasped mine. 'Jim was always speaking of yourself and Tom. You know, I can't believe he's gone, he was such a fine chap, a great lad.'

Amongst a huge congregation in Aberdeen, Tom paid a last tribute to his close friend. At the end of this moving address the mourners, mostly climbers from all over Britain, sang 'The Jolly Rover'.

Fergus was cremated in Paisley. His father, a retired engine driver and also a lover of the hills, thought it fitting that his son's ashes should be scattered in Glencoe, which Fergy had loved above all. It was a cold Sunday morning when we all met below my house at the Meeting of the Waters. Eric Moss had brought his pipes and the skirl of a lament rose above the roar of the river. The sun had risen over Beinn Fhada and was shining upon the west face of the Lost Valley. After 'The Flowers of the Forest' Eric played our own tune 'The Glencoe Mountain Rescue Team', which he had composed and Fergy always enjoyed, each in turn scattered some of his ashes into the white water of the Coe …

Mary Ann was buried in the quiet graveyard in Fort William. It was a bright, frosty morning, with the top of Ben Nevis gleaming a brilliant white and … the water of the loch glinting like quicksilver. Mary Ann had started winter climbing on one of our courses, where she also met Jim. She had an almost fanatical love for the Scottish Highlands, adopting this wild, mountainous region with burning enthusiasm. She must surely have had these hills in mind when she wrote these words in her song 'The Prawn Fishers',

> To the mountain tops, way up high,
> Take my hand love, by and by,
> We'll need the stars to guide us by –
> Come away now …

8   Clachaig Gully Rescues

I had been on rescues for many years in the Glencoe area, but my first rescue in Glencoe itself was in 1960, soon after I had come to live in the glen. Mr MacNiven was the owner of the Clachaig Inn at that time; he came up in his van to tell me that there seemed to be cries of distress high up in the Clachaig Gully.

Mr MacNiven was a unique character. He had a great respect for genuine climbers but, until he knew you, you were under suspicion. I can recall being in his small bar when a climber came in and asked for a pint of beer.

'Have you been up the hill?' was his quick rejoinder as he glared at the tentative offender. 'You don't look like a climber to me. That's not a climbing rope you have there; it looks like a washing line.' Indeed, at that time, some of the lighter climbing rope did resemble washing line. But Mr MacNiven had a heart of gold and he would do his utmost on a rescue. There were always flasks of tea and soup for the rescuers, and he himself, though not really fit for it and ill-equipped, would go up the mountains. His staff were never allowed to leave the hotel until the rescue party returned and had been served free meals. On one occasion, with old Mr Elliot – Walter and Willie's father – he spent the night with a body, high up on Stob Coire nam Beith, for at that time, the procurator fiscal of Argyll stipulated that no one was to leave the body of a dead climber until it had been examined by the police. That ruling, however, was quickly rescinded.

I followed Mr MacNiven down to the hotel and he pointed high up the gully, to a place where the growth of trees terminated; we saw a figure and heard faint calls of distress.

'You can see there, where the trees stop?'

Climbers had been attempting Clachaig Gully for fifteen years when in April 1938 Bill Murray, the well-known Scottish climber, found the key to the Great Cave pitch, which had thwarted previous parties, and made the first ascent of the longest gully on the British mainland.

The gully rises up from the doorstep of the Clachaig Inn in an uncompromising gash to the summit of Sgorr nam Fiannaidh, the western sentinel of the Aonach Eagach Ridge. It is not considered a good or hard climb by rock climbers but somehow it has a strange lure – probably because it starts so close to the road – and it must be climbed hundreds of times each year. In the spring there is an abundance of flora and in winter, when I was lucky enough to do the first winter ascent with a Creagh Dhu Mountaineering Club member, Bob Hope, it held a lot of surprises and difficulties, for the pitches above the Great Cave pitch were sheathed in ice and icicles hung over them, making the waterfalls resemble gigantic organs.

After the Great Cave, the next pitch of merit is Jericho Wall, a vertical, largely wet and greasy pitch of seventy feet. Above this the difficulties continue and escape from the gully is very difficult.

I set off up the hill with Mr MacNiven and a few volunteers, including Alec Foulton of the Creagh Dhu club, who went up the other bank. We gained a point above where the cries were coming from. It was a party of schoolboys who had got stuck; one was suffering from multiple fractures of the spinal column, arm and ribs.

With some difficulty I climbed into the gully, under a hail of boulders from the bank where some clumsy helpers were moving about. After many hours we brought the injured lad and his companions out and away to the hospital. Dr Donald Duff was at that time acting as locum to Dr MacKenzie, our local GP. Dr Duff was one of the great pioneers of mountain-rescue work in Scotland; he had started the Lochaber Mountain Rescue Team and had also designed and perfected the Duff Stretcher. He was a wonderful man, quiet and unassuming and completely selfless. The lad was sent to Oban Hospital for treatment.

In the meantime we both learned that the boys had been sent up the gully by their non-climbing master who had thought it a good day's exercise for them. They didn't know how to climb but had been throwing their rope over trees, then scrambling up it. Mr MacNiven's observations that they seemed to be 'where the trees stopped' held more than a grain of truth! The irresponsibility of this party's leadership was further illustrated when the master had the lad taken out of hospital two days later, despite the pleas of the hospital doctors. The boy stayed at a climbing hut for the rest of his holidays. Dr Duff's subsequent letter to the headmaster received a curt reply, stating that he should 'mind his own business' and that the school had many old boys who were very famous mountaineers.

On another occasion we were called out to rescue a person low down in the gully. In the late evening, as the long spring twilight eventually faded and the gully became a black slit in the hillside, I went up with Huan Findlay and Walter Elliot to investigate cries for help. Ian Clough and Jim McArtney went up the other side, as we were not sure from where the calls came.

Reaching a point about halfway, at the bottom of the Great Cave pitch, I went over the brink on a rope to investigate but couldn't see anything with my headlamp and received no response. Ian, on the wall opposite, was trying similar tactics.

Higher up, after two more abortive descents into the depths, there came an eerie cry from a branch of a tree nearby. I was almost startled out of my wits.

'Was that you, Hamish?' Ian yelled across.

'No,' I rejoined, somewhat shaken as I looked up at my nocturnal friend. 'It's a bloody owl – it has a mighty strange hoot!'

There was a further interesting episode in the history of the gully. One afternoon in August 1968 Dudley Knowles was in John McLaughlin's restaurant, which is situated on the main road near Glencoe village, when Jim McArtney came in.

'Oh, hello, Dud,' Jim called as he went to the counter to order a snack. 'You missed three good rescues!'

'I heard all about it,' said Dud (he obviously had not heard the word 'three'). 'It was only a little girl you took down from above the hotel; she slipped on the grass, or something.'

'Aye, she was one of them all right,' said Jim. 'But the other two were interesting enough.'

'What other two?' retorted Dud. 'Nobody told me about any other rescues.'

'The two in Clachaig Gully. We had to lower one chap by cableway.'

'Well I never,' said Dud indignantly. 'Why doesn't anyone tell me anything? There I was, sitting in that ruddy National Trust information van all day twiddling my thumbs and telling people where the bloody massacre was; and you up on an interesting rescue. Where was the other one?'

'In the gully as well,' said Jim, bringing his pie and chips over to Dud's table. Drawing a chair out he continued, 'One was below the Great Cave pitch and the other was above at the bottom of that short, hard slab pitch. He had fallen off the pitch.' Putting a loaded forkful of chips into his mouth, he added, 'I think that a piton came out and he fell down into the pool, injuring his back. The other bloke panicked and abseiled down the Great Cave pitch, only he forgot to fix a proper anchor for his rope!'

'Let's have the ruddy story from the beginning, Jim. Take a good swallow and let's hear the whole thing,' said Dudley, mustering his patience.

The story is as follows:

That afternoon Sandy Whillans had received a telephone call from Clachaig Inn. It was Jim, telling him that there had been an accident at the Great Cave pitch. Earlier that day the rescue which Dudley had heard about had been accomplished by Eric Moss and Jim.

Sandy could not get hold of any other members of our team. He forgot that Dudley was in the National Trust information van at a lay-by near Huan Findlay's farm. After asking some of his police team to meet him at the side of Clachaig Gully, he drove up to Clachaig.

'Jim has already left with a few volunteers and the stretcher,' one of the girls there informed him.

He climbed the path to the west side of the gully until, about halfway up, he found the easy track into the base from the Great Cave pitch. This is the only easy escape route from the gully as all the others are steep and loose. At the bottom of the pitch he saw Jim and two other climbers. At their feet, by the edge of a pool, lay the inert figure of the injured man.

In a few minutes Sandy joined them.

'This bloody stretcher is no use,' said Jim, looking up and flinging it to one side. 'It won't stay together.'

'You're no mechanic; that's MacInnes's latest model. Those two long lugs lock it in position once you unfold it.'

'I must say, I never thought of that,' said Jim, watching Sandy erect it. 'Damned clever, these teuchters!'

'How's the chap?' asked Sandy.

'Seems to have some bad head injuries; he doesn't look too good to me.'

The man lay unconscious on the casualty bag that had been placed under him.

'We'd better get him wrapped up and on the stretcher.' They put the stretcher alongside the injured man and, on a word from Sandy, lifted him on to it in one clean motion, in case he had further back injuries.

'All we can do is to lash him in now and wait for the others,' said Jim.

'How about someone going up to the edge in case my policemen arrive? They don't know the area very well.'

'I'll go,' volunteered one of the climbers.

The main police party were up shortly afterwards and ropes were sent down to haul the stretcher up the steep wooded bank, almost vertical in places. The path, which zigzagged up, avoided these sections but the stretcher had to go up by the most direct line: this was over steep, loose ground. Alasdair MacDonald, the gamekeeper from Altnafeadh, was at the edge and shouted down, 'Are the ropes attached, Sandy?'

'Not yet – in two minutes,' replied Sandy. 'Okay. Haul away, Alasdair, but slowly; there's a lot of loose crap about here.'

The stretcher rose by the concerted effort of ten strong policemen. When it was about twenty feet up, Jim shouted, 'Look out, Sandy!'

A large rock had detached itself from under the near-vertical turf and, apparently in slow motion, passed by the stretcher, taking a line for Sandy's helmeted head. Sandy got out of the way but he lost his pipe in the process!

I have always maintained that a good shepherd or gamekeeper makes an excellent rescuer. Not only have they a keen awareness of the limits of their capabilities and do not try anything harder than they know they can safely accomplish, but they have a high degree of common sense when it comes to first aid and care of the injured. I suppose they are so used to tending their stock and other sick or injured animals that they instinctively act correctly in a mountain emergency concerning human beings. This rescue was a case in point: as the injured man was pulled up to the lip of the gully, Alasdair noticed that he seemed to be making strange gurgling noises. In fact his tongue had fallen back and he was choking. In a trice Alasdair had forced his mouth open and pulled his tongue back again. This rapid action undoubtedly saved the man's life.

Some three years previously a similar situation occurred with a student who had fallen and was unconscious, with only minor head injuries. The rescue had been done 'on the quiet' by some of his fellow medical students. The tongue of this young man had also fallen back but none of his colleagues had noticed; consequently, he died about 100 yards from the main road, not half a mile away from Alasdair's house. I still shudder to think of the damage wrought by well-meaning 'do-it-yourself' rescuers with little common sense and no first-aid knowledge.

When the casualty had arrived at the top and some of the police had been detailed to carry him down to the ambulance, Jim turned to Sandy:

'I wonder where the other chap is. Have you any idea?'

'I suppose he must be up there somewhere,' Sandy nodded up towards the Great Cave pitch.

'We'll go up and take a look, shall we?' said Jim. 'Do you want a rope?'

'No, I think I'll manage all right; but I'll take one along just in case we have to come down sometime.'

They both climbed the Great Cave pitch, Jim leading. When he stepped on to the flat area at the top he saw the other climber lying on the stones beneath the following pitch – The Slab pitch – one of the hardest on the climb.

'Are you all right, lad?' asked Jim in his broad Aberdonian accent.

'Well, I've hurt my back; otherwise I'm all right.'

'Can you climb down if we give you a rope?'

'No, I don't think so,' the lad replied as he tried to stand up. He was obviously in pain.

Sandy took the walkie-talkie out of his pack and asked the police team members who were still watching on the bank, 'Have you another stretcher with you?'

Big Jim Brown, the policeman from Dalmally, replied, 'Aye, we've got everything but the Clachaig bar.'

'Fine. Take it to the base of the pitch, Jim – the stretcher, not the bar; we'll haul it up on the rope. Better take a spare rope with you too.'

Within half an hour the stretcher was at the base of the Great Cave pitch, unfolded and ready to be pulled up. During the intervening time, Jim had managed to get one end of their rope round a tree on the rock face some twenty feet above which is used regularly as an anchor. Sandy was now pulling the stretcher up on the other end of this rope.

The injured man was secured to the stretcher and the other rope attached to it; they then clipped two karabiners to four slings, the ends of which were knotted to the four corners of the stretcher, and finally the karabiners were clipped to the rope which hung from the tree. The end of this rope had been untied from the stretcher and went down to the bottom of the pitch.

'Hey, Jim,' called Sandy. 'Have a couple of lads pull the end of that rope out a wee bit and tie it round a rock. We'll use it for a cableway.'

'Right,' Jim Brown shouted back.

'We'll lower the stretcher using the other rope you sent up with it,' explained Sandy.

As soon as the suspension rope was tensioned they lowered the stretcher over the edge. Slowly the rope was paid out and, after swinging for a bit, the stretcher hung suspended on the slings with the karabiners acting as pulleys. It slid gently down the sagging suspension rope. This was the first time that any of the lads had fixed a cableway on their own and, with two men only at the top, it was no easy task.

The slow process of lifting the patient out of the gully had to be repeated all over again, but this time no large stones fell. Jim was down for his late afternoon snack by 4.30 p.m. after completing three rescues in the course of the afternoon.

A few years after this incident a young man from Cumberland fell, having climbed only a few feet up Jericho Wall. It was a Saturday night in early summer. I received the call at home and went down to the Clachaig Inn. The pub was mobbed by hundreds of thirsty weekenders and climbers. I found fifteen semi-sober climbers whom I knew, as for one reason or another most of our team were away. In the company of this inebriated group, many wearing their everyday clothes and shoes, we started off up the side of the gully. Denis Barclay was with a body of drunks who had insisted on coming and he realised that they could be an absolute menace on the mountain that evening. When persuasion failed, he chose the only alternative to a direct altercation: that of going up the hillside so fast that the unfit and the drunk fell by the wayside; the path was littered with mountaineers succumbing to violent bouts of sickness. He misjudged their determination, however, for one by one they doggedly continued the upward struggle, their faces almost as green as the grass surrounding the hotel below.

Walter and I managed to double-rope down to the injured man, while above us the noise of those being violently ill competed with the repartee of those still hale and hearty.

Bob Richardson, Ian Martin and David Crabbe – regular Glencoe climbers – together with our own men, Denis and John Grey, came into the gully behind us. After considerable trouble we succeeded in lowering the stretcher and casualty down the gully bed to the top of the Great Cave pitch. Meanwhile, we had contacted the cheerful team on the bank, then singing the 'Saqual Hail', asking them to descend and enter the gully below the Great Cave pitch where an easier entrance route lies.

We lowered the injured climber through space on a cableway to those below. He had a spiral fracture of his lower leg. I can recall quite vividly the stretcher as it ran down the cableway. Some of the drunks had infiltrated into the gully, despite an awkward descent from the bank, and the pull on the ropes did not quite coincide with the song that they were singing:

> We scraped him off the mountain like a pound of strawberry jam,
> We scraped him off the mountain like a pound of strawberry jam,
> And we put him in a bucket and we sent him home to Mum,
> And he ain't going to climb no more ...

With the uneven pull on the rope the stretcher rocked as it descended, although it was quite secure, for we at any rate were in possession of our faculties and at least two sober team members were below, keeping control of the exuberant helpers. We got the lad down and into the ambulance just before closing time, much to the satisfaction of the rescue party!

One of my part-time occupations is to survey possible climbs of the BBC Spectacular Live Outside Broadcasts. I do this work with Alan Chivers, who is the producer of these special events, Chris Brasher and Joe Brown. Joe usually has the role of star climber while Chris does the commentary. As there are considerable technical difficulties involved with some ventures, particularly from the mobile filming point of view, I advise and usually take charge of the rigging and also operate one of the portable radio cameras which are used on the climb.

Our specialised quartet has paid visits to mountain walls and pinnacles in various parts of the world; for every programme completed, about nine possibilities will have proved unsuitable. One of the major problems is transporting tons of expensive equipment and vehicles to within 5,000 feet of the intended climb – this is the maximum range, at the time of writing, for sending the signal back to the huge mobile control vehicle called the scanner, the heart of the unit. There are several TV monitors in the scanner which show the various pictures taken by the cameras at the climb. Alan Chivers's job is to select the best action shot and retain the viewer's interest – a task demanding split-second decisions. The TV signal may be sent out via various links to the nearest transmitter, which may be over 150 miles away, or it can be relayed by satellite.

In March 1971 I tentatively suggested a climb in Glencoe for one of these programmes. I told Alan that I very much doubted whether it would be within the 5,000-foot limit of the camera cable runs, but it was worth looking into it. Alan arrived in Glencoe during the evening of 1 April and over a drink at King House Hotel we discussed the project. I arranged to meet him at my cottage the following morning.

We both spent a full day on the steep face of Aonach Dubh, where the climb was located. It was a superb day and we found that the distance was, in fact, within the 5,000-foot margin. Alan was most impressed by the setting for the climb and, indeed, it would be hard to imagine a more ideal place for a live TV programme – an awe-inspiring vertical arena commanding views to the west over Loch Linnhe and Loch Leven, which lie beyond the village of Glencoe. The rigging problems were, however, extremely complicated. We would have to rely on helicopters for the major part of the project; this meant cutting a helipad out of the face of a rock buttress. Besides, a 1,200-foot cableway would have to be built right down the gully situated between the climb and the buttress, in case the helicopter was grounded due to bad weather.

On our way back we passed the time of day with Willie Elliot and then both made our way up the glen, stopping off at my place for a cup of tea. There was an RAF Mountain Rescue Land Rover in the lay-by opposite my house.

'Is there a rescue?' asked Alan.

'No, they're just up on exercise,' I replied.

I had a wash and changed, ready to go up to the Kings House for a meal, when there was a knock on the door. It was a member of the Leuchars RAF Mountain Rescue Team – one of the chaps from the Land Rover.

'Could I borrow a walkie-talkie?' he asked. 'Some of our party are overdue. They set off to climb Clachaig Gully, followed by a traverse of the Aonach Eagach Ridge.'

They were a party of two, it transpired, Tony Lawrence and Eric Henry, who were on a team-leader training course, and they had with them one of the RAF's walkie-talkies. I lent him my radio and he went off to see if he could raise his friends. Ten minutes later he came back.

'Can't get them, Hamish.'

'Oh, they've probably gone back down the other end of the ridge if they were delayed,' I answered.

I thought no more about it, as it is quite common for people to be held up in this long gully climb. But as I was leaving the house, some forty minutes later, Dudley Knowles telephoned from Clachaig Inn to say that he had seen a flare high up in Clachaig Gully.

'Can you ask Ann to call out the team then?' I asked. 'It looks as if we're in business.'

It seemed clear that the two RAF chaps were in trouble.

I joined Dudley at the inn. Ann, his wife, asked me if I wanted a plate of soup; I gratefully gulped this down while Dudley and his twin brother Dave put on their climbing boots. I asked Ann if she would contact the Kings House Hotel to tell Alan Chivers that I would be late and to start dinner on his own. Within a few minutes Willie and Walter Elliot arrived in our rescue truck, followed by Huan Findlay.

As we set off, I asked for a great deal of rescue equipment to be taken up, for it looked as if we would have to evacuate two men. From where Dud had seen flares, it was obvious that the party was very high up in the narrow confines of the upper gully; escape from this section is not easy, not only are the walls sheer, but they are loose and dangerous. As we walked up the carpet of grass at the bottom of the gully we passed a Land Rover caravette. A voice hailed me, 'Do you want any help, Hamish?'

It was Douglas Summers from Rhyl, who had been on one of our winter courses and was now on holiday.

'We could do with someone taking up a 500-foot rope.'

'Sure, I'll do that,' he agreed.

'Good, it's in the rescue truck.'

John Grieve had now arrived, despite having been suffering from a bad back all week. For days he had been sleeping on his face on the floor, so his young wife Elizabeth was somewhat surprised when he managed to get up after the call-out came through. I suggested, over the radio, that he should hold on at base for a bit to see what developed. Willie Elliot was to act as base operator on this rescue.

Just then I received a message from the injured party. This was indeed a luxury and the first time, that I can recall, that the victims had radio contact with the rescuers. We asked them to send up another flare to enable us to establish their location.

'Right. We'll send up a mini-flare in a minute. Afraid we'll both have to be taken out by stretcher – sorry.'

Soon we saw a ribbon of red climb out of the gully to explode level with the sides.

'Aye, it's above the Red Chimney pitch,' I calculated. (This is an awkward waterfall pitch high up the gully.)

'Yes, it looks like it,' said Dave, who was alongside me. 'It could be difficult!'

Taff Tunnah came over the radio. 'I got that message from the two lads, Hamish. Is there anything special you want taking up?'

'Hello, Taff,' I answered. 'Well, as you know, we'll need two stretchers, one right away and the other to follow. We'll also need two casualty bags and further first-aid equipment. Another 500-foot rope will probably be useful as well as some shorter ropes. We'll need pitons too, and pulleys and our two searchlights. Our team's a bit thin on the ground at present, I'm afraid, so we'll need plenty of help.'

'Wilco,' he replied. 'That's one thing I've got plenty of!'

We – myself, Dud and Dave Knowles and Chris Thomas, a regular helper with our rescue team – reached a point where we thought the climbers were, hidden in the 200-foot deep gash of the gully. Had anyone fallen from the edge, however, he would have dropped much farther than 200 feet, for the hillside is steep and the gully descends in a series of vertical steps. Later that night our searchlight was to drop into this abyss; it was recovered by a climbing party a few days later – some 500 feet lower, in pieces.

I contacted the two injured men, for I had to establish exactly where they were in case we knocked any stones down. I wanted to reach them from lower down the gully, not above them, for any dislodged stones, even if they did not hit them directly, might ricochet and be as lethal as shrapnel.

'Hello, Tony,' I called. 'Can you send one flare up vertically and another out horizontally so that we can ascertain exactly where you are?'

'Wilco. Give me a couple of minutes.'

The first flare broke out level with us and, seconds later, another could be seen shooting out of the gully horizontally and much lower.

'Okay, lads. We've got you pinpointed now.'

Dave and I moved on to a crumbly pinnacle which was attached to the side of the gully and tried to look down; it was not possible. The walls were too steep and appeared to overhang below.

'Let's get a belay, Dave, and I'll go down and see what's what.' Dave rummaged round the loose pinnacle and the only belay which was any use was one which encompassed it with a loop of the 200-foot climbing rope. I then eased my way down to the lip some forty feet below, from where I could look down and back into the gully where the two injured climbers lay. At this point, just above the Red Chimney pitch, the gully is very narrow, only a slit in places. Below me the two climbers lay on a stony shelf which is between two pitches. Both were in plastic bivouac bags and looked up at me in the fading light.

'How goes it? You certainly chose a difficult place!'

'Hello there, Hamish. Yes, it seems as if both of us will have to be taken out by stretcher. I appear to have bust my ankle and Tony here has back injuries.'

'Well, I'll have to go back up,' I called. 'Does this rope reach the bottom?'

'Yes, it just reaches down level with us. But you'll have to pendulum over when you get down because the rope hangs free over the next pitch below.'

This sounded ideal for they would be safe from falling stones. I called again, 'I'll have to go back up again and get things arranged on top. We'll see you presently.'

I quickly ascended the rope, using a jumar rope-clamp, and reached Dave and the other two. I explained the set-up. Huan Findlay and Walter had now arrived with Taff Tunnah, some way behind were the other volunteers. On the edge of the gully, a short way below, were the rest of the RAF party.

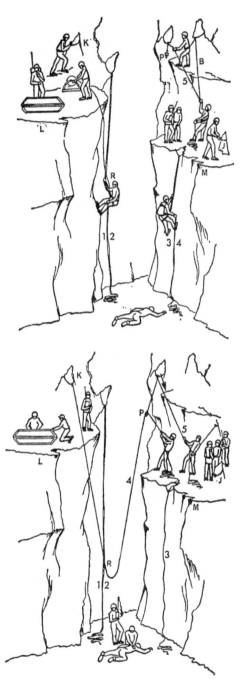

A Clachaig
Gully rescue

Rescuers abseil down from
each side of the gulley on
doubled ropes 1–4. Left
one takes rescue rope R.
Ledge L: Rope R paid off
drum and end secured to
belay K. Stretcher prepared
for lowering with
suspension slings and
pulleys. *Ledge M*: Sling
placed for pulley on end of
rope 5. This rescuer is
safeguarded by rope B. He
returns to ledge M with
pulley. R attached to 4
and pulled up to ledge M.
4 and end of R pass
through pulley.

Rope 5 tensioned, so pulley P moves into required position. R taken through rope clamp J. Abseil ropes 2 and 3 taken up to ledge L and attached to ends of stretcher. Stretcher pulled out to centre of gully and lowered.

Once stretcher has been pulled up to the required elevation it can be taken across to either ledge.

'It looks like a complicated evacuation,' I told them. 'It could take us ages to get them out of the gully by lowering them down the pitches, but to try and pull them directly up would be folly, for the sides of the gully are dangerous and huge loose boulders could be dislodged by only the slightest touch.'

With this fact in mind, I suggested an angled cableway which would take the injured party diagonally out of the gully to the true right, or left, bank. It was just possible but would rely on being able to find good belays in the bed of the gully, while the line of the evacuation would have to be clear of the gully walls. I turned to the radio again and asked John Grieve if it would be possible for him to come up, for we were lacking in technical knowledge.

By this time it was almost dark. The sun had set, glowing like a great peat fire, and across the glen Sgùrr na h-Ulaidh was silhouetted in the bright light of the moon. It was a wonderful moon which was rising and it provided our main source of light for the next seven hours. I thought of Alan at Kings House and said to Dave, regretfully, 'Well, by this time I should have been well sated after an excellent hotel meal.'

'Never mind, Hamish,' said Dave. 'It'll do you good to fast. All this soft living will get you down.'

'Not much hope of that – living in Glencoe!' was my retort.

We established a slightly better belay and I prepared to go down. I didn't want more than two people in the gully as someone might easily be injured. I abseiled down first, taking with me the first-aid equipment, splints and personal gear. As I eased my way down I could pick out the light of the Clachaig Inn, 1,500 feet below. At various points beside the gully there were pencils of light, indications of other rescuers. I was hanging free now and somehow my headlamp wire became entangled in the abseil rope. The farther I descended the more wire passed through the abseil karabiner, causing the elastic head-band to stretch. It had reached a stage where the strain on my neck was becoming unbearable; I couldn't flick it off my head for I was in a tricky position: after travelling through space some distance I was hanging near the end of the rope, just touching the rock. At this point I had to swing in towards the two injured lads. With my head almost through the karabiner clip I dropped on to the scree ledge with a gasp of relief.

As soon as I had regained my composure I contacted Dave.

'Okay, Dave. You can come down. I'll hold the rope over for you to save you having to swing at the bottom.'

Dave's silhouette appeared against a moonlit sky. It was a wonderful sight: behind him the peaks to the south of Glencoe were bathed in moonlight, the tops still white from the winter snow, and ice glinted in the gully below. Meanwhile, talking to Tony and Eric, a glance had assured me that any equipment we had to ease their predicament was superfluous; they seemed to have everything. Though they were cold, both were well wrapped up and established in the best possible place on the ledge.

When Dave joined me I gave Tony some painkilling drugs and looked about for suitable belays. Dave had brought down with him the end of a 500-foot rope. We hoped to use this end for the proposed cableway. Upon investigation, the bed of the gully proved to be devoid of suitable belays, while pitons would not be adequate to take the strain in the particular direction necessary for a cableway. On a small ledge above the others, I sat down and thought about the problem. Suddenly the technique which I had worked out for an accident while I was on Crowberry Ridge the previous New Year came to mind. Why not here – the situation was ideal? Joining Dave, I broached the subject.

'Remember that technique which I thought of for the Crowberry rescue, Dave? It would be possible to use it here.'

'That really complicated thing? Well, I suppose it has to be tried out sometime. I'm sure the lads here don't mind being the raw material for your experiment, furthering progress and all that,' he laughed.

Tony and Eric seemed unimpressed and Tony asked suspiciously, 'What exactly do you propose to do with us?'

I told them in the least dramatic way possible that it meant lifting them by a stretcher on a rope which was anchored at the top of the gully on one side, came down to the stretcher and through two pulleys which would be attached to the stretcher by four slings, then up the opposite side of the gully to some of the rescue party on that side. As this rope was taken in and ran through the pulleys the stretcher would be raised. Two further ropes would be tied to each end of the stretcher; these would be held by parties above, one rope at either side of the gully, for extra haulage and safety. All three ropes would be taken in simultaneously so that the stretcher and its passenger would travel straight up to a point midway between the tops of the gully walls – once there it could be pulled to one side or the other.

The main difficulty at this moment was that no one else on the rescue was familiar with the technique. The only others who knew anything about it were the people actually on Crowberry Ridge with me that night, besides John Grieve and his wife. Liz, John's wife, had been helping me to illustrate a book, *International Mountain Rescue Handbook*, so I had explained the system in detail to John; he then helped Liz by explaining it to her for the illustrations. Fortunately, John was now at the top and in radio contact with me.

'Hello, John; hello, John; come in, please.'

'Reading you loud and clear, Hamish.'

'John, do you remember the series of drawings Liz did on the gully evacuation – the ones I worked out for the Buachaille rescue?'

'Yes, I think so,' said John, thoughtfully.

'Well, I suggest that we use that method tonight; it seems the only logical way. But it will mean you going over to the other side of the gully to establish a first-class belay; without that we're sunk.'

'I can do that okay, but I'd better take John Hardy, Walter Elliot, Dudley Knowles and Huan Findlay with me as well; there are enough RAF chaps this side now. We'll have to cross the gully some way above, then descend the other bank to this level.'

'Fine. I'll hear from you in due course. Don't forget to take a rope.'

'Hello, Taff,' I called over the radio. 'Come in, please.'

'Receiving you, Hamish.'

'Taff, I'm going to relay to you the procedure for doing this particular technique. It's a bit complicated so I'll take it slowly.' I explained in detail how the operation was going to be done and, when I had finished, I asked if he had understood it all right.

'There are one or two points, Hamish. The first is: I have a set of the lightweight winch pulleys made up, similar to the ones you have; should I use this winch system for hauling up one of the ropes?'

'Yes, you can if you wish. But if you've enough men there you can just apply manpower to each of the ropes to keep the operation as simple and fast as possible.'

'I would like to try it, though.'

'Fair enough then,' I replied. 'Provided it doesn't hold us up. I have the end of the 500-foot rope here which Dave brought down. As soon as John Grieve's party gets to the other side and they put their rope down, I'll tie the end of it to the rope end which you will lower down to me shortly. You will then be able to haul it up so that you will have the end of John's rope as well as your own rope. You can tie the ropes to either end of the stretcher as safety ropes. The stretcher will then be ready for lowering down into the gully, suspended from the pulleys on the 500-foot cableway rope.'

Within an hour or so John and the rest of the Glencoe party had made their way across the gully much higher up and they were now descending the true left bank. We could hear them above us; the ring of pitons being driven into cracks in the rock broke the still of the night. Dave and I chatted with the two RAF lads. Eric was feeling the cold, for it was a frosty night. We were also cold and hungry but, sheltered from the wind, eventually we dozed peacefully while our friends were busy on top.

'Rope coming down,' John's voice rang out from above; he was close enough to shout. 'Where exactly are you?'

'Just throw the end straight down and we'll see if we can spot it, John.'

'Right. Here she goes.'

In the beam of our headlamps we picked out the rope end, hanging to our right in the shadow of the left wall of the gully.

'Try again; about twenty feet to your right.'

The rope disappeared up over the vegetated gully side.

'Coming down again.'

The end whistled past my ear, sending a few small rocks crashing to the pitch below.

'Right, we've got it,' yelled Dave.

'Tying on the end of the 500-foot rope now,' I shouted. 'Haul it up.'

The end of the long rope started to move upwards to John's party and soon it was hanging in a great parabola from one side of the gully to the other.

'We've got it tied off on to a belay now,' John's voice came over the radio.

'Fine. Can you send down the end of your 200-foot rope again? Just put a weight on it and slide the end down on a karabiner clip, with the clip attached to the suspension rope.'

'We're lowering it now. Let us know when you get it.'

'Fine,' Dave shouted. 'Got the end.'

'Okay, John,' I repeated over the walkie-talkie, in case he hadn't heard. 'We have it now and we'll join it to the end of Taff's 200-foot rope.'

'Listening in, Hamish,' said Taff.

'Hello, Taff. We've got them joined to it. You can pull up your 200-foot rope now. Have you got the stretcher rigged for coming down next?'

'Yes, everything's ready here; we're just making the final adjustments to the stretcher slings for attaching the two pulleys.'

'That's grand; we'll only fix up the one stretcher, using it twice to get the lads out, and put each patient in a casualty bag. This means that the first man up will be transferred at the top to another stretcher, while the second man can stay on the gully stretcher till he reaches the road.'

'Aye, that seems sensible, Hamish. We're now tying the two rope-ends to each end of the stretcher. As soon as we clip the stretcher pulleys to the suspension rope I'll get in touch with John and he'll be able to pull the stretcher out into the middle of the gully where it should hang from the pulleys on the 500-foot suspension rope.'

'I'm receiving all this,' said John. 'Just give the word.'

'Well, we're ready for launching,' said Taff. 'There are two casualty bags on the stretcher and I think that the stretcher should hang okay.'

'Great, can you start taking in, John?'

John's rope tightened so that it now ran parallel with the suspension rope which had been taken in by Taff's party; presently the outline of the stretcher showed up clearly against a white cloud.

'It seems to be going fine,' I said. 'Like clockwork. Take it out for about another sixty feet, John. Taff, you can start lowering the suspension rope and your 200-foot, slowly and at the same time. It may as well be going down as it comes across.'

The stretcher started to descend, well clear of the rock walls, and not a single stone fell. Only the slight squeak of the suspension pulleys could be heard, and the muffled shouts from above as instructions were being given.

Eric and Tony gazed up at the stretcher.

'Christ!' said Eric. 'What have we let ourselves in for? This isn't a rescue – it's a bloody circus act!'

'Ah, it'll just be like floating on air,' rejoined Dave consolingly.

In a matter of minutes the stretcher was a few feet above our heads.

'Take it slowly now,' I told Taff. 'You've only six feet to go.' The descent rate slowed right down with the precision of a dockyard crane.

'Right. That's it; we have it on the gully bed. Slacken off.' The ropes slackened and the stretcher lay at our feet.

While I made some further adjustments to the stretcher suspension slings, Dave took the casualty bags off the stretcher and laid them out on the boulders. We put the men in their respective bags; next moved Eric on to the stretcher, lashing him in securely; then asked Taff to take a little tension on the suspension rope. When this was done the stretcher was suspended about eight inches above the gully floor, hanging from the suspension rope on the two pulleys.

'All seems well down here, Taff. We're ready to go, but a word of warning before we start. All three ropes, the suspension rope and the two which are attached to the two ends of the stretcher must be taken in simultaneously; this will avoid excessive strain on any one rope. If I see any of the ropes going slack I'll immediately let you know, but you'll know yourself by the feel of the rope. When the stretcher reaches a point high up, almost level with the edges of the gully, you must avoid putting too much strain on the suspension rope. It has a breaking strain of only 3,000 pounds and will be near its limit.'

'We got that,' said Taff.

'Okay,' said John. 'Say when.'

'All together, now,' I said.

In a series of small movements the stretcher started to ascend, maintaining a perfectly horizontal keel. Its path lay on a central vertical plane between the gully walls. Every thirty feet or so there would be a short check as Taff reengaged the pulley-winch system which he had attached to the suspension rope.

In fifteen minutes the stretcher had risen 150 feet and I was becoming anxious about the strain on the suspension rope. I told Taff to start taking more strain on his stretcher rope, just in case the suspension rope broke; had this occurred, the stretcher would have been securely held between the two other safety-haulage ropes, but I naturally didn't want it to happen. A few minutes later I urgently repeated the message, now much more worried; from where we were in the gully, looking directly up at the tiny bleak outline of Eric on the stretcher, the suspension rope seemed to have diminished to the diameter of a thread with the strain, so that it was difficult to pick it out. I was relieved to hear Taff's voice.

'We're taking it across now. Sorry, we were very busy when you last called; there were a few problems.'

'I'll leave you and John to arrange getting the stretcher to your side now, Taff. I can't very well direct it from down here, anyway.'

'That's okay,' John came in. 'It should be straightforward.'

'Slacken off, John,' said Taff. 'And we'll pull it across.' The stretcher moved horizontally to the west side of the gully and came to rest against the gully wall, just short of the brink. It was quickly hauled up out of sight by the men.

I breathed a sigh of relief. 'Well, it worked, Dave. Thank goodness!'

'Just a treat,' said Dave. 'What a sight! Funny how all these dramatic things happen at night when we can't get a photograph. If we had a cine camera down here we could have got some fantastic shots.'

'Well, at least we didn't have to work by searchlight,' I replied, pointing at the moon. 'This has been the best lighted rescue for many a day.'

'Hey, look at this ... ' He held up some clothes pegs he had found on the gully floor.

'What on earth are these doing here?'

'They don't belong to us,' said Tony. 'We don't use them.'

'Perhaps someone took them up to get handholds on thin rock ribs,' I ventured.

'Yes, and you can use them instead of rope clamps to get out of this ruddy place,' retorted Dave.

Soon the stretcher was making its second journey down. We strapped Tony firmly to it.

'Have a good trip, Tony,' I said. 'Think of us, going up the rope out of this hole.'

On the given signal the stretcher started its ascent. Again, everything worked like a piece of well-oiled machinery. Less tension was applied to the suspension rope on this occasion but, when the stretcher was hauled up over the lip, one rope was found to be frayed almost through. It must have been running over a very sharp rock on the edge. This demonstrates the punishment to which equipment is subjected on actual rescues. Frequently the 500-foot ropes only last one rescue before they are scrapped. The three ropes used on this call-out were retired afterwards because they were overstrained and mutilated.

The rope leading from the stretcher end to John Grieve's party was the best rope left; it was removed from the stretcher and dropped into the gully. I then started to climb it, using jumar clamps, besides partially climbing up the steep gully wall by using my feet. In a few minutes, after a struggle past some overhanging loose rock, I joined John and the other lads at their belay.

'We'll be in time for breakfast,' said someone. 'Or at least, we'll have coffee in our truck.'

'Has someone told Willie to put the kettle on?' asked John Hardy.

'We soon will,' returned Walter, picking up the walkie-talkie. In about ten minutes Dave was with us and we coiled up the 200-foot rope and dropped the end of the 500-foot rope down from the belay into the gully. It was then pulled up and coiled by the RAF party on the other side of the gully.

The remainder of the RAF Leuchars Mountain Rescue Team was now taking the two casualties down using long back-safety ropes, for the going was steep on the west bank. On the walkie-talkie I heard Taff ask his control vehicle to contact their base at Leuchars for a helicopter to come and pick up the two lads to take them to hospital. Taff's station, RAF Leuchars, Fife, is also the base for the rescue helicopters under the Northern Maritime Region; they were then using Mk 10 Whirlwinds.

In the cold grey light the glen looked sombre. The moon had done its night's work and had gone to rest; a low mist hung over Loch Achtriochtan. The smoke from the chimney of the Elliots' house rose straight up in the still air.

We ran down the hillside, glad to get the blood circulating again. In the rescue truck we had coffee and Guinness, while the Argyll county police truck arrived promptly with further supplies of hot drinks and soup.

A short way behind us, coming down the final slopes, were the two stretchers carried by the main rescue party. To the east, as the first shaft of sunlight touched the pinnacles of the Aonach Eagach, the drone of a helicopter could be heard. It had come over the snow-covered Highlands across Loch Tummel and Loch Rannoch – the Road to the Isles – and landed in Glencoe near the Clachaig Inn. The pilot, Flight-Lieutenant Keith Fitton, flew the two injured lads back to RAF Leuchars in an hour and they were then taken to Dundee Royal Infirmary. Both were out climbing again in a matter of months and were eventually none the worse for their experience.

9 Ted Nowak's Flying Circus

The climbs which we chose for the Glencoe live TV programme were two of the hardest in Glencoe: *Hee-Haw* and *The Big Top*. Joe Brown was going to partner Chris Bonington on *The Big Top*, while two climbers from Edinburgh, Dave Bathgate and Sophia Houston, would climb *Hee-Haw*. I proposed to cut helipads on the steep buttress opposite the climb and to build huts and cable-ways there to cope with the necessary equipment. Over 15,000 feet of one-inch-diameter camera cable, which weighed one pound per foot, had to be carried down the face. Another 20,000 feet of a different cable had to be positioned as well.

The helicopter company with which we originally arranged this contract proved quite unable to accomplish it. As a matter of fact, the pilot never got anywhere near the helipad. Chris Brasher, refusing to be daunted, came up with an alternative.

'I know a pilot,' he asserted, 'who will land his machine on a flagpole.'

At the time, I laughed at this optimism; subsequently, I revised my opinion: nothing seemed impossible for Ted Nowak when we got to know him. He was a quiet, unassuming chap, more like someone you would expect to meet in a city office than a highly skilled pilot, but on our very first flight together he landed on the helipad with one skid balanced on the edge and the other hanging in space. While he was doing this, the rotor was only a matter of two or three feet away from the sloping rear wall of the ledge.

Despite the adverse weather conditions right up to the last minute – we even had snow – the programme went well. As the sun came out the glen glistened like a freshly painted picture and the climbs, although they were much more difficult when wet, provided spectacular television viewing. Afterwards we had the whole de-rig of the programme planned like a time and motion study, so that the helicopter could be used to its maximum and enable a number of the vehicles to get away to start other scheduled programmes. There was also a further reason for urgency: Ted's wife was due to be admitted to hospital for an operation and he had to be present to provide his signature.

The morning of 1 June dawned fine and clear. As soon as breakfast was over at Kings House Hotel, Ted flew down the glen in the Alouette and we sent up all the BBC staff in groups of three for the de-rigging of their equipment. The work continued in the afternoon without a hitch. Alan Roberts and I took it in turns to fly with Ted, advising him on pick-ups from the various sites and helping him to marshal the helicopter into the gully where equipment was being lifted directly instead of being taken back to the helipad above, which would have entailed considerable delays.

After a few trips, during which he got the feel of things, Ted flew right to the base of the climb, the helicopter rotors revolving only inches away from the great rock wall as he lifted out cameras and electronic equipment, much of which was more valuable than the helicopter itself. Most of this delicate apparatus was taken down that day, and we finished just before the sun dipped down in a great wreath of fire over Garbh Bheinn in Ardgour.

In the morning we were back at the Elliots' field; it was now being cleared of vehicles and gear. Ted ferried up my instructors and some more of the rescue-team volunteers who were helping in a last drive to clear the hill that day. Several climbers walked past our landing site in the Elliots' meadow and continued on foot on the path which leads up to Bidean nam Bian, the highest peak in Argyll. This was a common enough expedition and one which attracted little attention. One of these men, however, was not to come down again alive.

Most of the work had been completed when Huan Findlay, Willie Elliot and Brian Wright – a friend of Huan's who had been helping us – decided to call it a day; Huan had cattle to feed and other work to do on his farm. On their way down they passed a climber slowly descending; although this did not strike them as unusual at the time, it later transpired that he was actually on his way down to raise the alarm for an accident high up on the face of Bidean nam Bian – it didn't occur to him to tell anyone about it on his way down.

'Well, cheerio, Willie,' said Huan. 'I'll see you later.'

'So long,' Willie shouted in return as he entered his cottage. A few minutes later the chap they had seen on the path above knocked on the cottage door.

I was just about to jump into the helicopter with Ted to pick up another load from the helipad when Willie rushed out and waved to me.

'Hamish,' he called. 'There's been an accident on Bidean, up by the Church Door Buttress. Can you have a look on the next trip?' After I had obtained a more precise location, I set off, shouting as I passed to Huan Findlay who was just about to drive off in his van, 'Can you come up with me, Huan? There's been an accident.'

Huan never refuses a call for help and without a moment's thought – typical of Huan's trust in his fellow rescuers – he threw his shepherd's stick to Brian and leapt into the helicopter.

I explained the situation to Ted and he agreed to fly us up and see what could be done. As soon as the engine reached its correct temperature, Ted took off; he asked me further questions regarding the accident, over the headphones.

'I don't know much about it, Ted,' I replied. 'All I know is that a chap has fallen to the side of Church Door Buttress on Bidean – that peak up there,' I pointed towards it, 'and that he is seriously injured. If we can just go up and ascertain the situation, we could leave Huan up there. There's a landing site on the top; he might be able to reach either the fallen man or his companion, who, I gather, is stuck. I will have to stay with you to continue with the de-rigging.'

'If he only has a broken leg, or similar injury, Hamish,' said Ted, 'we can take him in the Alouette, but a serious injury requiring a stretcher could be more complicated. I have no fittings on the skids for taking a stretcher.'

'Fair enough,' I answered. 'We'll see what the position is shortly.'

We were rising quickly now; in front of us the great twin buttresses of Bidean nam Bian loomed black against the last of the winter's snow which encircled them. High up on the ridge, to the right of the summit, a solitary figure stood looking down at us.

'This is Church Door Buttress here, Ted,' I pointed. 'That other buttress on the left is Diamond Buttress. The injured chap must be somewhere to the right by the edge of that snow. I gather he fell down a small chimney.'

Although all three of us were used to searching from helicopters, we didn't spot anything as we flew up past the face of the buttress.

'How about landing on the summit, Ted? Over there.' I pointed to the left. 'It seems a good place.'

'Sure, we can do that easily,' he answered confidently, although a nasty summit breeze was blowing up from the south-west.

'Give us a signal when it's all right for us to jump out, will you?'

'All right,' he replied, concentrating on bringing the machine down on to the rough ground on an even keel.

Bending low, I waited for his nod: the reason these machines are called 'choppers' is that you can lose your head at this particular stage if you don't bend low and rapidly move out of range of the rotors while within the pilot's field of vision. There is also the danger – though more often encountered when shutting off power – of blade-sailing: the rotors may dip down to a point very close to the ground, with fatal results if you happen to be in their path.

Huan followed quickly after me and we went over to the edge of the face, keeping within shouting distance of each other, and looking down the snow slope. The solitary climber whom we had seen on the ridge came across to us and, although we couldn't hear his shouts very well for the noise of the Alouette's engine, he pointed down at an angle across the snow slope to where, presumably, the climbers were. I shouted to Huan. 'Huan, I'll leave you here and go and have another look with Ted; then we'll pick up Sandy from the F Buttress helipad.'

'Okay,' he shouted, waving a hand.

I dashed back to the helicopter and, once strapped in, put the headset on and spoke to Ted. He started to take off.

'It looks as if the injured man is at the top of that big scree slope we looked at coming up, at the snow line. Can we have another look on the way down, just to make sure?'

'Yes, of course, Hamish,' his voice crackled over the phones. 'We'll take it more slowly this time.'

The tall figure of Huan became smaller as Ted side-slipped the helicopter down into the corrie.

'Can't see anything down there, Hamish. Can you?'

'No,' I replied. 'Not a thing. We'll take Sandy Whillans up on the next trip, if that's all right by you?'

'Yes, we can get Sandy up next if you want,' Ted answered, now taking a direct line back to the landing field. 'Is there anything else you need taken up?'

'We'll take the first-aid rucksack next trip,' I suggested, adding, 'we don't want this interruption to interfere with the de-rigging programme, Ted. There are too many people involved in it and it will cost the BBC a lot of money to hold things up.'

'Yes, it is a problem,' he answered thoughtfully.

When we landed I discovered that Willie had contacted the party above at F Buttress helipad and Sandy Whillans was already there, standing by to be picked up.

'I've asked Ted to take Sandy up now,' I yelled to Willie. 'We still haven't found the injured man.'

'All right,' called Willie. 'I'll hold on here.'

I went back to the helicopter and we flew up to the helipad again, the engine note reverberating from the face behind. We saw Sandy standing beneath the helipad, clutching a walkie-talkie. He had no other equipment. Meanwhile, all work on the de-rigging operation had come to a standstill as nothing more could be done until the helicopter was free. I directed Ted into the helipad and, as soon as the machine had one skid touching, gave Sandy a nod to come aboard. Once Sandy was strapped in I equipped him with a set of headphones and told him what had happened to date.

'You'd better take this small pack with you. There's some first aid in it,' I told him. 'If you need more we can bring it up with the stretcher.'

'That's fine,' he replied. 'You say the fallen man must be at the bottom of the big snow slope?'

'It's the only place he can be,' I answered. 'Anyone falling down from the edge of Church Door Buttress on that side is bound to fall down the snow slope.'

'We'll have another look on the way up, shall we, Hamish?' suggested Ted.

'May as well, he must be there somewhere' I rejoined.

The helicopter swung in low over the scree at the foot of the buttress and slowly climbed up, parallel to the slope and about ten feet above it. It was a brilliant exhibition of flying on Ted's part, for a sudden down draught during this manoeuvre would have been extremely dangerous.

'Can see a ruddy thing,' said Sandy in disgust.

'He must be there somewhere,' I stressed. 'Will we drop you off at the top so you can go down the slope and join Huan?'

'That'll be fine,' Sandy agreed.

'Jump out when I give the okay,' instructed Ted.

'Aye,' said Sandy, taking up the pack in one hand and handing his headset back to me.

Once again, Ted landed on the summit; in a couple of seconds Sandy was well clear and giving us a farewell wave.

'We'll take one more run down this snow slope,' Ted's voice came slightly distorted over the headphones.

'He must be there,' I assured him. 'But there doesn't even seem to be a mark on the snow, it surely can't be so hard at this time of the year with the sun on it?'

Bidean nam Bian, 3,772 feet, is the highest peak in Argyllshire; the corrie into which we were now dropping like a stone forms a natural bowl. In Ted's expert hands the machine skimmed down the steep snow slope at what seemed to me to be an alarming speed. Yet, despite the rapidity of our descent, Ted had the machine on a level keel in an instant when we reached the area where we knew the man must be.

'Look there,' he pointed (though how he saw anything amazed me). 'Two climbers!'

Sure enough, two climbers were making their way up the large scree at the foot of the long snow slope and we could discern an orange blob immediately above them – the fluorescent anorak of the fallen climber who was lying prone across a pointed boulder. Above him, some 600 feet higher, we could now make out a figure in a blue anorak; this, we concluded, must be the survivor. Away to his right the large, spreadeagled form of Huan Findlay could be seen, like a fly on a whitewashed wall, making his way down towards the distressed climber who was at the bottom of a short rock chimney.

'Any chance of landing near here, Ted?' I asked, pointing towards the fallen man.

'We'll try,' was his brief response.

I could see him taking everything into account: the wind, the angle of the slope, which was very steep, and at the same time eyeing a large boulder, the size of a bus, on which he could rest a single skid while I jumped out.

'I'm taking her in, Hamish. Take care with the rotor,' he added. 'It's mighty close to the rocks above.'

I saw what he meant: the rotor seemed only inches away from the top of the next boulder up the slope; any sudden movement downwards of the helicopter would have been disastrous.

I grabbed some first aid which was lying on the floor of the helicopter and waited for his nod. A full twenty seconds had passed before I received it. His eyes never wavered from the ground directly ahead. I had marshalled him down so that the port-side skid just rested on the side of an enormous rock where he held the machine by feel, watching his instruments and a fixed point ahead of him.

I jumped out as soon as I received his signal. He could not take off and wait for me because the landing was too difficult to do on his own, so he remained where he was, hovering above me, while I climbed out on the side where there was greater clearance from the rotor. I had no desire to find out whether there was room to crawl below the rotor and the boulders above – I was certain there wasn't.

I reached the injured man just behind the two climbers and quickly examined him. He was an oldish man, lying face down. I asked him how he felt and he appeared to be able to speak normally, but when I asked him to try to move his legs he was unable to do so. His spine was obviously broken, and, as his head was turned back at a very strange angle, I was almost sure that he also had a broken neck. I knew that if I tried to move him he would probably die – he would probably die in any case, I realised, but I had no stretcher and not enough people to lift him on to one, even if it had been available.

Spinal injury is one of the biggest headaches on a mountain rescue. Usually we move a climber with a spinal injury according to the way he is lying; that is, if he is lying face down we put him face down on to the stretcher, using four trained rescuers to lift him in unison at a given signal and place him gently on the stretcher; he is then secured in that position. Most mountain-rescue medical experts advocate that casualties should be moved only face downwards and there seems to be a strong case for this advice.

Sadly I turned away. There was nothing I could do for him. Had he suffered less-severe injuries we could have got him aboard the Alouette and completed what would probably have been the fastest rescue in the history of Scottish climbing; but I knew it would be fatal to move him.

'Don't attempt to move him until we get a stretcher,' I told the two climbers.

'We'll bring more help shortly.'

I then returned to the helicopter. Once aboard, Ted took off with obvious relief, for he had had a hard time keeping the machine stationary in such a difficult position. I explained that I couldn't move the climber, whom I later discovered was named Charles Esslemont Ross (it was his sixty-second birthday that day), because of the severity of his injuries, and asked Ted if he would return to the Elliots'.

I was now faced with a difficult decision. We had to finish the de-rig: a large number of scheduled vehicles were still awaiting equipment from the helipad and there were many people working at both ends of the helicopter run, depending upon it to clear off the mountain. Besides, we could not delay the operation another day since the weather might break at any time and leave us in a serious dilemma, as we had about 15,000 feet of heavy and valuable cable, costing £1 per foot, on the mountain. Moreover, Ted's wife was needing to go into hospital fairly urgently.

I broached the problem with Ted.

'Ted,' I began. 'If we make one more flight with the stretcher we could then get back to the BBC job. I don't know how it will work out financially but I feel sure that the BBC won't mind the expense. When we land I'll ask for an RAF helicopter to be sent to pick the man up from the corrie; it won't be too difficult for the lads to take him down there. How does this plan suit you?'

'Yes, I think that'll be all right, Hamish. It's a pity, though, that we can't take the man down ourselves.'

'Yes, it is,' I agreed. 'But he would have died, I'm afraid.'

'Where exactly do you propose that the RAF Whirlwind should land?' asked Ted.

I pointed into the bowl of the corrie directly below us. 'On those flat rocks there, Ted; there should be plenty of room, don't you think?'

'Oh, yes, there won't be any bother. Flying conditions are excellent at present.'

Having taken the helicopter round on a sweeping circuit of the corrie, Ted now took it down through the gap between the shoulder of the west face of Aonach Dubh and An t-Sron and landed a few minutes later in front of the Elliots' house. By this time PC Ian Gillies from Kinlochleven, one of Sandy's assistants, had arrived, so I asked him to contact police headquarters for an RAF helicopter, and to inform the local doctor of the accident.

While I had been coordinating the various sections of the rescue operation, flying up and down in the helicopter with Ted, Huan Findlay was directly involved in the situation as it developed on the hill. He himself gives an account of the early stages of the rescue:

> As my friend, Brian Wright, had to go back to Liverpool that night, we finished at the helipad earlier than the others and set off along the path about four o'clock; Willie was with us. As the helicopter continued its shuttle service, ferrying equipment back down the mountain, we all three wished we could have had another flight, though we knew this was impossible because of the tight time schedule.

We were approaching the Bidean corrie, where the path bears right to descend and eventually to join up with the access path to Bidean nam Bian, when we saw a figure – a young man, obviously a hillwalker. We kept a parallel course with this youth who took the true left, or west, bank of the Bidean stream while we took the easterly side. He was only a short way off as we slowly descended.

When we reached the house this same chap met Willie at the door of his cottage, just as we were saying 'Cheerio'.

'There's been a serious accident on Bidean nam Bian,' he said. 'A man has fallen down beside the big buttress on the right.'

'Church Door Buttress?' asked Willie.

'Yes, that's right,' replied the lad.

'Why didn't you tell us when you saw us up in the corrie?'

'I never thought,' returned the lad.

Willie dashed into the house to telephone the police; then came out and rushed over to Hamish who had just landed with Ted Nowak, the helicopter pilot. He hurriedly told Hamish what had happened. In a few minutes Hamish came over to where I was standing with Brian.

'Huan,' he began, 'would you like a short trip to the top of Bidean to see if we can spot this chap? Six eyes are better than four.'

I looked at Brian to see if he minded.

'Of course not,' he replied promptly. 'I'll still be at the farm when you get back.'

I didn't even bother to take my crook and I was dressed in the minimum of clothing, for it was a sweltering day. As we climbed up through the narrow gap between An t-Sron and the west face of Aonach Dubh, the great snowfields of Bidean came fully into view and it grew much colder. Though I studied the area to the west of the Church Door Buttress as we climbed, I could see no sign of the fallen man, or of his companion, who was, we understood, uninjured.

I heard Hamish speaking with Ted over the headphones, asking him if he could land on the summit. Before I knew what was happening, Hamish was saying that we should get out as soon as Ted gave the signal. I bent low, following Hamish over to the edge of the face which overlooked the main western snow slope.

We had a look over it but couldn't see anything. He suggested that I should stay up there and he would go down and pick up Sandy Whillans so that we could climb down together. A chap who had been waiting on the ridge then came across and, when the noise of the helicopter had died away, he was able to tell me that he had seen the accident happen and then pointed out precisely where the uninjured climber was.

It seemed to me foolish to wait up there until Sandy came so I started to go down to the edge of the snow and then began to cross it in a long traverse. At this point I certainly got a surprise for, under about half an inch of soft, slippery slush, the snow was very hard indeed.

'Oh gosh,' I thought. 'This is a bit tricky.'

I had to kick the edge of my boots through the soft cover of snow into the hard underlayer and, with my fingers held rigid and vertical, I drove them into the snow to enable me to hold on. I wished then that I had my crook or ice axe. It was a long way to the bottom of the snow slope and I didn't want to join the fallen climber involuntarily.

At a point below a rock chimney I found the climber who hadn't actually fallen. He was in a crevasse which had formed between the rock and the snow. Clad only in shorts and a pullover, he was shivering violently; obviously he was in a state of shock. He was uninjured and was too frightened to move, which was probably just as well as he might easily have joined his companion, who was somewhere down the long snow slope below us.

He told me that he was a novice and was being taken out by Charles Ross, who had some twenty years' experience of climbing in the Scottish hills. He had mentioned to his older companion that he wasn't very happy – they didn't seem to have the equipment for such an excursion. But, like me, they didn't expect to find hard snow on such a hot day in June. He didn't say too much, however, for he was, after all, a mere beginner. He followed his companion, therefore, who had by this time forsaken the hard snow for the rock chimney above us, which he then proceeded to climb. He watched Charles as he ascended, allowing him sufficient time to get up this awkward-looking section before he followed.

'Suddenly,' he related in a shocked voice, 'Charles slipped and hurtled past me. He hit the snow, then accelerated down the steep slope at great speed.'

Apparently he didn't hear any cry from below. He shouted for help and a man on the ridge – the one who met us as we jumped out of the helicopter – waved to him.

I started to take him down the slope, keeping to the margin of the snow where we could get some positive holds on the scree at the edge. When we were a little way down, Sandy suddenly appeared from above. We hadn't even heard the helicopter return, though in fact it had passed quite close by. After a few words, Sandy continued on down the slope in search of the fallen climber. In about fifteen minutes we joined up with him again.

Charles Ross was obviously in a critical state and I think that he must have been very close to death then. I decided to return back up the slope and collect some of their gear which we had seen strewn about on the fall. While I was halfway up the snow slope, picking up various items of clothing, I saw the helicopter return to the party below.

Meanwhile, Ted and I had loaded a stretcher into the helicopter and I had a brief consultation with John MacCaw, the only BBC man of authority still on the site. John agreed with me that we should do what we could within reason and use the Alouette for a further trip with the stretcher, since this was vital for the rescue.

A few minutes later we set off, taking with us further first-aid equipment and the casualty bag. As we approached the location for the third time we could see signs of activity quite clearly. Sandy had managed to get down from the summit to the injured man and was waving to us.

Ted took the machine in with considerable speed and very little marshalling help from me; he laid one skid against the boulder as gently as the bows of a ship touching a pier in the hands of a competent skipper. I quickly threw out the casualty bag, which caught, unfortunately, in the down-draught of the rotors and was blown down on to the rocks below. The stretcher and first aid were put out without difficulty, although a large container of DF118 tablets, which we sometimes carry instead of morphine, fell also; the container of tablets was scattered by the turbulence amongst the vast boulder field.

As soon as the task was completed we pulled away without delay and once again I breathed with relief, for it was nerve-racking to remain in that hazardous position. In about two minutes we were back at the field, where Ian Gillies came over to say that a helicopter from RAF Leuchars would arrive in just over an hour and that an RAF team from St Asaph, who were on exercise at Kinlochleven, would be coming round to marshal it in.

I continued to discuss the routine for the remainder of the de-rig with Ted, while keeping in touch with Willie and Ian Gillies, since both men were in radio communication with Sandy and the helipad people.

'Hamish, a message from Sandy,' called Willie presently.

'He says that he thinks the chap has died. Would you go up once more to confirm this?'

Dr MacKenzie, our local doctor, had been informed of the accident but was out on another case.

'Well, I suppose I could,' I replied reluctantly. Like Sandy, I had experienced the complex business of determining death many times; no single layman likes to accept such a responsibility. A first-aid card written by my wife, Dr MacInnes, emphasises the gravity of such decisions:

> DEAD: The question of death can be very difficult in some cases. If there is any doubt, artificial respiration and/or external cardiac massage (by pressing firmly and regularly on the breast bone) should be carried out until signs of death are clear or breathing starts again. Nearly all the commonly used signs of death, e.g. no pulse, apparently no breathing, muscular rigidity, pale 'dead-looking' patient, can occur as a result of a drop in body temperature. Unless the victim has injuries obviously incompatible with life, it would be wiser to treat as alive until expert medical opinion is obtained. The 'apparently dead' person is in much greater need of urgent assistance than his injured companion – with say a broken leg. Remember the gravity of the decision when you decide someone is dead. When somebody dies blood drains into whatever happens to be the lowest parts, producing a bluish-red stain in the skin. It will not be present over areas subject to pressure, e.g., if lying on back, staining will be present at back of neck, and small of back, but not over shoulders and buttocks. This staining may be confused with bruising but with bruising there is usually localised swelling and possibly skin abrasions.

Sandy's predicament was not an enviable one, Huan didn't want to commit himself. He had no alternative but to ask my opinion, for what it was worth. I knew, however, that if Sandy thought he was dead, then he would be, for we always play safe. We have heard of too many mistakes in the past. From time to time, even with the extremely rigorous controls in hospitals, one reads of patients reviving in mortuaries, although this is now, fortunately, a very rare occurrence.

Sandy had asked for some ropes so I loaded these on to the stretcher before we took off. Some of our regular rescue team had now arrived and already Dud Knowles, Walter Elliot, Rory MacDonald and Mr Moncrieff, Walter's employer, who helps us from time to time, had set off. We soon passed them as we shot upwards and I felt sorry that they had to walk; but there was no alternative since I couldn't authorise the extra flying time. Already the bill for the BBC was mounting steadily.

Ted performed his boulder-embracing technique again – for the last time – and I jumped out, as careful as ever. Ted took off and rose a few feet in the air, hovering; obviously he was finding it too taxing to remain poised upon the boulder. Quickly, I went through the mechanical motions of trying to detect signs of life. Like Sandy, I was convinced that the climber was dead, but a hope that there was a glimmer of life still persisted, so I suggested that we should treat him as live and evacuate him to the corrie for the pick-up by the RAF helicopter. In our game one cannot afford to take chances with life: it could easily be our own some day and we, I feel sure, would wish to be treated as alive until there was obviously no more hope.

Once more we took to the air and went directly down to the helipad, where we collected a load and carried it down. From then onwards, we continued with the ferrying of equipment, only pausing to refuel from time to time.

At 5.50 p.m. the yellow form of the RAF Whirlwind appeared. It had taken an hour and ten minutes to travel from Leuchars in Fife. I went over and had a word with the winch man. As he approached me I recognised him, for he had helped us on previous occasions. I gave him the map reference of the pick-up, telling him that the stretcher party was already there and awaiting them. He gave a nod and immediately took off, for the pilot had not switched off the engine. Slowly, compared with the Alouette, the Whirlwind gained height; then it disappeared like an enormous yellow moth, into the depths of the corrie.

Ted and I had meanwhile brought another load down and he had reached the final stage of ferrying down the personnel from the top by the time the Whirlwind reappeared. Dr MacKenzie from Ballachulish had arrived and drove up to the RAF ambulance which had picked up the climber, a short way from the Elliots' house.

'Oh, he's dead all right,' confirmed the doctor. 'He must have died pretty quickly with those injuries.'

The next day we managed to remove the remainder of the camera cables from the gully. Ted was now on his mettle and on each trip was lifting three 200-foot cables, weighing 600 pounds. As the gully was extremely narrow in places, with not enough room for the rotor in its deeper sections, we had to put a long nylon rope extension on to the hook wire. It was a fascinating and exciting experience flying into the depths of No. 4 Gully and lifting out three 200-foot lengths of cable on an extension of eighty feet. The end of the nylon rope extension was clipped to the middle of each group of three cables; then Ted took the Alouette up vertically. While this was being accomplished, the climbers in the gully – Alan Fyffe, John Grieve and Kenny Spence, helped by Ian Nicholson and Rab Carrington – would run like mad, if one can call moving over the almost vertical rock walls of the gully running, as the top section of the cables bounced downhill, sending boulders in all directions, and the lower section of cables rose upwards. I had to watch both ends simultaneously to ensure that there was no major snag which could affect the stability of the helicopter.

It was an education to us all of what could be achieved by an expert. I suppose that Ted also felt he was with experts and in this he was right, the lads down below, who seemed to move like chamois on the steep terrain, were some of the best mountaineers in Britain.

By late afternoon the next day, somewhat behind schedule, we had taken all the BBC equipment off the hill. We were so exhausted that we could only sink down on the grass in Willie's field as Ted's mechanic refuelled the Alouette. Ted came over to us and shook our hands.

'Well, chaps,' he remarked in his quiet, unassuming way, 'it's been a great job. It makes a change from flying high-powered film stars about!'

He was dressed in a large, thick overcoat and wore, as usual, his soft hat with a pheasant feather sticking out at one side. He looked more like a bus driver, just off duty.

'Sorry I won't be able to complete an honorary circuit before I leave, but the old girl,' he pointed affectionately towards the Alouette, 'is so full of fuel that she'll take offence if I try anything fancy for at least an hour.'

I went over to the machine with him and bade him a last farewell.

'I'll be up in Glencoe again, Hamish,' he said. 'I'll bring my son up here next time; it's a wonderful place.'

He took off then, as soon as the helicopter was warmed up and their belongings were stowed aboard. The Alouette rose slowly above the loch, reflected in its inky depths, as it began the long journey back to Oxford. Ted's visit will long be remembered by the rescue team in Glencoe, for he had opened new horizons to us in the art of flying.

The Conquest of Buachaille Etive or The Orra Lad's Tale

by E.A. Balfour

When wintry blizzards come and go
Aboot the peaks o' drear Glencoe,
And guid folks huddlin' roond the peat
List tae the blatterin' o' the sleet,
It's then ye'll hear the story told
Hoo long ago in days of old
Twa orra lads, sae rins the tale,
Did michty Buachaille Etive[1] scale.
God kens the stock frae which they sprang
But they were souple lads and strang,
For no anither since that day
Has ever climbed yon fearsome brae.
The first ane's name, or sae I'm told
Was John MacSnorrt, and he was bold,
A tall, camsteerie, ugly chiel
Wha's temper was the verra de'il.
The ither's name was Wullie Flyte:
At little man wha's build was slight,
His shanks were thin, his hands were wee,
An inconspicuous lad was he.

At Kingshoose Inn they spent the nicht
And started off at dawning licht.
Eh man! but it was sad tae hear
Hoo yon MacSnorrt wad curse and sweir:
'De'il tak ye, Wulliel Hurry up!
Ye're like a muckle daunderin' tup.

---

1. The exact position of this hill is doubtful. Offenbach puts it in MacGillicuddy's Breeks, but this is improbable.

Ye're not tae taigle us, d'ye see,
We maun be back in time for tea.' [2]
So off they went wi' highest hopes
And sune had climbed the gentle slopes,
And as they left the darksome glen,
Before them rose the michty ben,
Steep precipices, fearfu' chasms,
Eneuch tae gi'e the bauldest spasms.
'D'ye think,' speired Wullie, "we micht fa"?' [3]
MacSnorrt, he answered nocht at a',
Juist boond a rope about his wame
And made puir Wullie dae the same.
They made quite sure it couldna slip,
And, each an ice-axe in his grip,
They started up, hand owre fist,
There was nae crevice that they missed,
Nae handhold but was firmly grasped,
Nae slabs but they were safely passed,
And mony a steep and icy gully
That put the fear o' God in Wullie.

At length MacSnorrt got on a ledge
Abune an awfu' chasm's edge,
And Wullie, scrambling doon beneath,
Cried up tae him through chatterin' teeth:
'I hope that ye've belayed yersel'.'
but bauld MacSnorrt juist answered: 'Hell!
Man, but ye're gettin' awfu' saft,
The folks that use belays are daft,
Belays, ye ken, can only gie
A sense o' fau'se security.'
Wullie replied: 'Well, if I fa'
It's your fau't.' John said: 'Not at a',
It's yours for being sic an idjut,
Noo be a man and dinna fidget.'

---

2. This was considered almost a point of honour by some mountaineers.

3. There is evidence throughout the poem that Flyte must have had English blood in him.

Sae Wullie, baith his e'en shut ticht,
Climbed up the rope wi' a' his micht.
And wi'oot further hesitation
Achieved at length his destination,
And clung there safe wi' pantin' breath,
His cheeks were white wi' fear o' death.
And noo sae far up had they come
There nocht was left but an easy lum,
Up which they went wi' ne'er a slip
Tae reach the mountain's lofty tip.
They sat them doon tae rest a bittie,
Says Wullie: 'Man, isna that pretty?
Peak upon peak sae fair and grand
Like elfin towers in fairyland.'
MacSnorrt said: 'Dinna be sae fulish,
There's naethin' there but Ballachulish,
For God's sake dinna get poetic,
It acts on me like an emetic.'

Tae a' guid thing there comes an end,
The 'oor has struck, they maun descend.
MacSnorrt, for tae show off his skill
Sets oot glissadin' doon the hill.
But pride aye comes afore a fa'
For what he thocht was frozen snaw
Was really ice, and sune he slippet
And lost the ice-axe that he grippet.
Upon his back at furious pace
He shot twa hundred feet through space,
And on his doup he landed fair,
Eh! but yon dunt maun hae been sair.

Wullie cam clamberin' doon richt fast
And reached the stricken lad at last
Man, but it gi'ed him joy in troth
Tae hear MacSnorrt bring oot an oath,
And then in muffled accents ask
If Wullie had the whusky flask.

He seized upon the braw Glenlivet,
And though I ken ye'll no believe it,
He didna draw a breath nor stop
Until he's finished ilka drop.
It filled puir Wullie wi' vexation,
He got quite red wi' indignation.
MacSnorrt juist wiped his muckle mou'
And scrambled up. Man, he was fu',
He clutched at Wullie lest he fa',
He couldna stand his lane at a'.

Puir Wullie didna breath again
Until they reached the level plain,
But noo the world was lost tae sicht
In darkness o' approachin' nicht,
And mony weary miles were passed
Afore they reached the door at last.
The landlord welcomed them wi' joy
Tae see them safe frae sic a ploy,
The guidwife sune was on her feet
Tae get them a' a bite tae eat.

Oh happy man am I tae tell
That merry evening a' was well.
The table sune was neatly laid,
And steaming dishes were arrayed,
And though MacSnorrt declined a seat –
He took his supper on his feet –
His aches and pains were quickly drooned
As bottles travelled roond and roond,
And Wullie sune was heard tae say
Hoo much he had enjoyed the day.

But ane and a' agreed tae this:
While perfect rock is perfect bliss,
And ringing axe is music sweet,
The simpler joys are hard tae beat.

Acknowledgements

I should like to thank the many people who have helped me by supplying valuable information without which I would have been unable to write this book with any semblance of accuracy. Their assistance has enabled me to reconstruct the following rescues from various angles, seen through the eyes of both rescuers and 'victims'.

I should also like to thank the BBC for the use of tape recordings which I made during interviews, and several of the police authorities for assistance both with my researches and in helping me to locate elusive rescuers who had long since hung up their rucksacks.

Finally, as the original manuscripts of this book were destroyed in a fire, I should like to thank Miss Elizabeth Whittome for her patient help in transcribing the final text from illegible notes.

Willie and Walter Elliot.

Sandy Whillans.

Huan Findlay.

Denis Barclay.

Eric Moss.

Team members.

Glencoe.

Rannoch Moor.

A fatality.

Above: Lifting a casualty from Shibboleth on Buachaille Etive Mor.

Right: The Great Gully avalanche: two doctors try to revive Gunn Clark with oxygen and cardiac massage.

Below: PC Kenny MacKenzie with his rescue dog.

Ian Clough.

Derrick Grimmitt (*Dalness Gully* rescue).

Fergus Mitchell.

Jim McArtney and Mary Ann Hudson.

Members of the Glencoe Mountain Rescue Team wait to lower a casualty on Buachaille Etive Mor at night.
L–R: Ronnie Rodger; Sandy Whillans; Davey Gunn; Larry Taylor; Nigel Stafford; Huan Findlay; John Grieve; Dave Todd.

Crowberry Tower, Buachaille Etive Mor. **1** Indicates the South Ridge up the *Crowberry Tower* (CT). The bivouac site
is just to the right of the *South Chimney* (SC). **2** Is the normal route up to the summit of Buachaille Etive Mor.

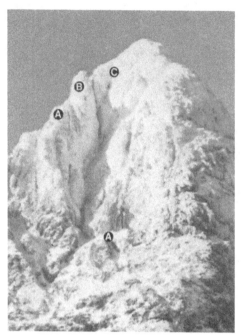

Buachaille Etive Mor. A and A show the span of the cableway. B is the bivouac site. *Crowberry Gully* is between the As. *Rannoch Wall* and *Curved Ridge* are to the left of the top of A. C is the point the party fell from on the 1,000-foot fall to a point out of sight on the lower continuation of *Crowberry Gully*. The dark slit is *Raven's Gully*, leading into *Great Gully*.

Ben Nevis from the air with the peaks of Glencoe in the background. The top **X** indicates where the slab avalanche started and the lower one the place where the bodies were recovered. The Charles Inglis Clark Hut is indicated by the **H**, and the drop-off point in the valley which the helicopter reached is marked with a **D**.

Training exercise with a MacInnes Mark 3 stretcher.

The cliffs of Ben Nevis from the Charles Inglis Clark Hut. The summit is top left of the picture and **X** marks the slab breakaway point. **A** indicates the avalanche debris where the three climbers were found. **GT** is the Great Tower of Tower Ridge and **DB** is Douglas Boulder. This 'boulder' is 700 feet high.

Part of the Black Cuillin Ridge, Skye.

The Bidean nam Bian massif, Glencoe. Above the Elliot's cottage on the left is Aonach Dubh. The arrow indicates the summit of Stob Coire nan Loachain. To the right of centre is Bidean nam Bian with its twin buttresses. To the right again are Stob Coire nam Beith and An t-Sron. It was near here that part of the Massacre of Glencoe took place. **1** is East Buttress, where the *Big Top* climb is located. **2** is the helipad.

153

Ted Novak in his helicopter. **B** indicates the summit of Bidean nam Bian, with Church Door Buttress directly below the summit.

The view from the Allouette on the day of the rescue. **H** is the point where Huan Findlay and Sandy Whillans were dropped off. **D** is the *Diamond Buttress*. **C** is *Church Door Buttress*. **R** shows where the fallen climber lay and where Ted Novak landed the helicopter. The dotted black line indicates the line of fall from higher up the buttress.

Printed in the USA
CPSIA information can be obtained
at www.ICGtesting.com
JSHW012016140824
68134JS00025B/2456